When Lincoln Met Wisconsin's Nightingale

Cordelia Harvey's Campaign for Civil War Soldier Care

Daniel L. Stika

When Lincoln met Wisconsin's Nightingale Cordelia Harvey's Campaign for Civil War Soldier Care
Copyright © 2020 by Daniel L. Stika

Library of Congress Control Number: 2020917407
ISBN-13: Paperback: 978-1-64749-235-9

All rights reserved. No part of this publication may be reproduced, distributed, or transmitted in any form or by any means, including photocopying, recording, or other electronic or mechanical methods, without the prior written permission of the publisher or author, except in the case of brief quotations embodied in critical reviews and certain other noncommercial uses permitted by copyright law.

Although every precaution has been taken to verify the accuracy of the information contained herein, the author and publisher assume no responsibility for any errors or omissions.No liability is assumed for damages that may result from the use of information contained within.

Printed in the United States of America

GoToPublish LLC
1-888-337-1724
www.gotopublish.com
info@gotopublish.com

Cordelia Harvey stands in the company of great women, who, when convinced that their cause was just and right, worked tirelessly to achieve the ends they desired. Due to her passion for the care of soldiers fighting in the American Civil War, the lives of many were saved. These soldiers were then able to return, which eventually resulted in the ending of the war. Her passion and courage are to be admired and emulated by the women of today.

Dedication

Innumerable scholars and historians have long established that death during the American Civil War reached into the world of the living in ways that were unknown to the American public. Disease, along with infections, due in part to reprehensible environmental conditions in the hospitals and the battlefields, caused the most deaths. This book is solemnly dedicated to everyone who made a valiant effort to correct this situation and helped save the lives of the soldiers during this tumultuous time, especially Cordelia Adelaide Perrine Harvey.

Acknowledgments

Although the author's name appears on the cover, it is God who takes the plaudits. He must be thanked for providing the strength and fortitude it took to complete this project. As the to-do list piled up higher and higher and there seemed to be no end in sight, he was the helping hand through all of the stressful times.

It is sometimes stated that with ordinary people, most achievement is concerned with the embellishment of one's own ego; mine is no different. Therefore, I am increasingly conscious of the fact that if there is any success to be had, it is due mainly to those who have instructed me. The failures, then, if any, are mine alone.

Table of Contents

Foreword 13

Introduction 17

The Civil War Medical Dilemma 23

Abraham Lincoln:
Leadership and Character Analysis. 47

Cordelia Harvey:
Nineteenth-century Humanitarian 67

Harvey's Campaign Strategy for
the Union Soldiers 87

Conclusion: Theoretical Analysis 107

Bibliography. 119

Endnotes 127

Foreword

Abraham Lincoln was known for his persistence. He did not allow personal grief, financial difficulties, and political disappointments to stop him from becoming one of the most revered and sagacious leaders in American history. Contemporaries noted his insistence on getting to the truth, his powerful analytical abilities, and his willingness to concede points to opponents if they had valid arguments to make. In seeking results he considered right, he often reached conclusions slowly and carefully. "Besides his well established reputation for caution, he was concentrated in his thoughts and had great continuity of reflection," recalled his long-time law partner William Henry Herndon. "In everything he was patient and enduring. These are some of the grounds of his wonderful success."

Lincoln frequently advised others to persevere when they had a setback. One such occasion occurred when his son Robert told him about his friend George C. Latham not being admitted to Harvard. Lincoln, who was a few months away from being elected president in 1860, wrote to the young man that he should keep trying and not be discouraged by a "temporary failure" in the great struggle of life. "I know not how to aid you," he wrote, "save in the assurance of one of mature age, and much severe experience, that you cannot fail, if you resolutely determine that you will not."

Lincoln's life became a model for American striving and doing. (One of Horatio Alger's popular books was Abraham Lincoln, The Backwoods Boy; Or, How A Young Rail-Splitter Became President.) His life, like Benjamin Franklin's, was mythologized and memorialized in the nation's civil religion. Men who exemplified the virtues of hard work and public-spirited achievement could become icons in the country's historical memory and imagination, but women with similar struggles and accomplishments were often forgotten.

In the nineteenth century, a person's gender determined expectations about careers and even many rights, including suffrage. Yet, while they were denied full citizenship and career opportunities beyond basic labor tasks, women were able to participate in reform movements, write books (such as Harriet Beecher Stowe's Uncle Tom's Cabin), and initiate civic improvement projects of many kinds. During the Civil War, as in the later world wars, women had a chance to show what they could do in responding to the greatest of national challenges, massive and devastating armed conflict.

When Lincoln met Wisconsin's Nightingale: Cordelia Harvey's Campaign for Civil War Soldier Care is a fascinating, informative book about two persistent people and how they debated the issue of where Union soldiers should be hospitalized. One was President Abraham Lincoln, who was besieged by citizens who wanted his help. The other was a woman who went to the White House to argue her case for a change in how casualties would be treated. Cordelia Harvey, the widow of a Wisconsin governor, confidently confronted a man known for his debating skills. Daniel L. Stika's account of their lives and encounters gives us fresh perspectives on how Lincoln could be persuaded and how a woman of the Victorian Age could act when others were in peril.

—Professor Jeffery A. Smith,
Department of Journalism and
Mass Communication, University of
Wisconsin—Milwaukee

Introduction

Physicians, politicians, and military leaders had to cope with rampant camp diseases and overwhelming battlefield casualties throughout the progression of the American Civil War (1861–1865). Attaining success in the struggle against infection and injury was extremely crucial to the war effort, but decision makers had only rudimentary understandings of effective medical treatment.

Critical issues regarding proper medical care during this period have long been debated. In 1861, the United States Surgeon General's office consisted of 115 surgeons, twenty-four of whom resigned to form the nucleus of the Confederate Medical Service. The two armies, being quite inadequately expanded, relied on both male and female nurses, many of whom were not sufficiently trained, but above all, most of the nursing service was voluntary. Walt Whitman, considered to be one of the greatest American poets, served as a volunteer male nurse in the hospitals.[1]

Numerous hospitals lacked the requisite qualities or resources to meet the task. Inspections of Union Army hospitals in 1862–63 found 589 suitable and 303 unsuitable. While inspecting the medical officers, 2,727 were found to be acceptable and 851 deemed unacceptable. Antiseptics were relatively unknown, and the relationship of dirt to infection was not fully understood by the medical personnel. Anesthesia was just coming into general use, while a number of the available drugs were considered deficient.

An enormous number of these existing circumstances added to the seriousness of many procedures, particularly surgery. As bad as Civil War surgery might seem, diseases and infections were frightfully worse. Scholars, looking at Civil War medicine in hindsight and comparing it to a world of medicine that was born many years after 1865, refer to it as one of the biggest failures of its time.

Although she was not a nurse, Cordelia Harvey did invaluable work for the soldiers. She did not contribute anything of substantial value toward medical knowledge, but her persuasive techniques as a lobbyist and activist were of immeasurable benefit to the Civil War soldier.

Innumerable people were either directly or indirectly affected by this dreadful experience during this tumultuous time. The Harveys however, were totally committed from the very beginning. Cordelia eventually became directly involved after her husband's tragic death.

Harvey, being in the midst of the wounded and ill soldiers, was able to relate some of these horrendous conditions to the president and the officers that were under his command. The book cover depicts the seriousness of the situation. The wood background represents the tables that the soldiers would have had to lay on for operations. The gauze, thread and needle help to emphasize the crudeness the soldiers had to endure. This, then, is an in-depth glimpse into a relationship between a president and a very resolute woman determined to change the state of health care for Union soldiers.

Historical evidence shows that she was at first rebuffed and had to make numerous visits to the White House to share her plight with President Lincoln. He, along with a number of military generals, staked claim to the assertion that many soldiers would desert if allowed to leave the battle zone.

Cordelia has understandably been envisioned as a very strong-willed, highly intellectual person. She was a leader, not only by virtue of being a schoolteacher, but also her demeanor prior to, during, and after the war.

Nineteenth-century women were beginning to realize that there were considerable opportunities for them outside of the home. Feminism was being born, and traditional views of women were changing.

Women, as has been noted, definitely wanted to vote, work, and go to school. Middle-class life would be changed dramatically.

Harvey, after accepting an appointment and serving in the capacity of a sanitary agent for the United States Sanitary Commission, saw what the conditions were like for the Union soldiers at the camps and in the hospitals. Having fallen ill while visiting the Wisconsin soldiers in the South, she was rushed back to her home in Madison, to recuperate. It was during this interval that she wrote President Abraham Lincoln, requesting funding for northern hospitals.

A character analysis of Lincoln reveals that he was known to have had a dark side. He was disturbed by hints of treason or treachery. Defeatists exasperated him, generals disappointed him, colleagues conspired against him, newspaper articles depressed him, and many of his friends died during the war. Lincoln had been estranged from a shiftless father and had a woeful marriage to a woman who embarrassed and at times physically abused him. He sometimes displayed a streak of cruelty, an explosive temper, and an aversion to women. Harvey's persuasive efforts were aimed at a man who could be harsh and distrusting but also compassionate.

Achieving success in her encounters with the president, Cordelia was present when the Harvey United States Army General Hospital opened in Madison. The hospital was used as a convalescent hospital for wounded soldiers able to withstand the difficult journey north.[2]

Reliance on an understanding of the horrific circumstances of Civil War medical care, along with a perceived character analysis of Lincoln, were major influences in Harvey's persuasive tactics. She definitely recognized the burdens placed upon his shoulders. Cordelia had to overcome his negativism and still justify her requests so that a mutual understanding could eventually be reached.

A number of scholars have made various references to this remarkable woman. Many have also suggested that there is a great deal of scholarly literature, specifically about her, that should be cited regarding her humanitarian contributions on behalf of the Union soldiers. It has also been noted that no one has focused on how she was able to change the minds of such powerful men, including the president of the United States.

This book expounds in great detail on how she was able to persuade President Abraham Lincoln to provide funding for northern hospitals. Even though she was regarded as a strong-willed, highly intellectual woman, and a great deal of insight on Cordelia Harvey's work for the soldiers is shared with the reader, one must be cognizant of the fact that nineteenth-century women were still suppressed to some extent.

Realizing what the issues were brings to the forefront some of the more obvious questions that will be examined and answered. How then was this nineteenth-century woman from Wisconsin able to overcome President Abraham Lincoln's vehement objections and persuade him to fund northern hospitals for the Civil War soldiers? What techniques did she use to garner support in her campaign for the Civil War soldiers? Why was this woman so unrelenting in trying to convince the president that her suggestions were the right thing to do for the health and welfare of the soldiers? Where did Cordelia Harvey meet with President Lincoln to discuss her strategies? How often did she have to meet with him? When did Cordelia finally realize that she had accomplished her long sought after quest? What was the end result of this long and tenacious campaign that she undertook on behalf of the Civil War soldiers?

The Civil War Medical Dilemma

Denouncing the Civil War's medical problems as one of the most problematic failures of the war has been, and still remains, a contentious issue. When comparing the collective medical knowledge of the mid-nineteenth century to that of the twenty-first century, one could logically conclude that the standards of health care and the skills of the providers were quite poor. Dr. William A. Hammond, surgeon general during the war, claimed, "The Civil War was fought at the end of the medical Middle Ages."[1]

There are many historians who have even suggested that aspects of medicine were more primitive in nineteenth-century armies than in the armies of antiquity. Author Stewart M. Brooks stated, "For all intents and purposes, the doctors and apothecaries of the 1860s knew scarcely more about drugs than did the physicians and priests of ancient times."[2]

Widespread conceptuality of Civil War hospitals and doctors evoked vivid pictures of bloodstained surgeons performing amputations at the rate of fifteen an hour amid piles of limbs and of amputees and convalescents crowded into hospital wards. According to Brooks, there was some truth to these images. Wounds complicated by badly broken bones nearly always resulted in amputations, and amputations were always followed by an infection. Disinfectants were seldom utilized in hospitals before the war. Surgery, today the paradigm of cleanliness, did not become aseptic until Ernst von Bergmann introduced steam sterilization of instruments and dressings in 1886. In 1891, he introduced aseptic methods to the practice of surgery. In 1890, Dr. William Halsted introduced the use of thin rubber gloves that did not impede the delicate touch demanded by surgery. By ensuring more sterile conditions in the operating room, Halsted's gloves allowed surgical access to all parts of the body.[3]

Civil War surgery has been depicted as atrocious; however, diseases were frightfully worse. While it would be difficult to say that typhoid fever or chronic dysentery was worse than a penetrating gunshot wound, it can be said with certainty, according to Civil War historian James M. McPherson, "that disease was worse in terms of the numbers of soldiers killed outright, or rendered unable to fight. Microbes killed more men than bullets at every stage of the war, and no regiment was safe from epidemic diseases."

Still, as high as the two-to-one ratio of death from sickness versus death from combat might seem, a two-to-one ratio of disease to combat death was not surprising in its historical context. It was, in fact, better than the ratio for other nineteenth-century wars. In the Mexican and the Spanish-American wars, the ratios were seven-to-one and six-to-one, respectively.[4]

Collectively, in society as well as in the armed services, disease has been much less of a problem in present times because of bacteriology and modern drugs. Equally important to the prevention of disease is proper hygiene and sanitation. The science of bacteriology, which is common medical knowledge in the present time, was relatively unknown throughout the medical community prior to the Civil War.

Louis Pasteur (1822–1895) founded the science of microbiology and proved that microorganisms cause most infectious diseases. This later became known as the germ theory of disease. Another contributor, Joseph Lister (1827–1912), worked on the development of antiseptics and clean surgery to eventually kill any bacteria that was getting into the wound from the air. Their peers did not generally accept the scientific works of both Pasteur and Lister until the 1870s, though they began in the 1860s, and their new theories would not have a major impact on medicine until the end of the 1800s.[5]

Extremely high rates of disease in the army were understandable, in that the existence of bacteria was still a mystery, but neglect of sanitation was also at the root of the disease problem. Military officers wrongly assumed that volunteer soldiers were up to the rigorous discipline required of regulars. This, combined with the rugged individualism of the majority of soldiers, created a hygienic nightmare in camps that encouraged the spread of lethal diseases. Doctors, unmindful of common measures of sanitation, were also responsible for numerous deaths from infection.

Dr. William W. Keen, a surgeon from the United States Medical Department, wrote in 1918, "It can easily be understood, now, how and why we surgeons in 1861–65, utterly unaware of bacteria and their dangers in our innocence, committed grievous mistakes, which nearly always imperiled life, and often actually caused death."[6]

The world will never know to what degree this was true. Hospitals too were under the leadership of an inadequately prepared army medical department. They were centers of infection, contrary to their inherent purpose. Essentially, rates of disease and the number of deaths from diseases were higher than they might have been had proper attention been given to preventative measures.

Attempting in any way to excoriate by pointing out real or perceived flaws of the medical mind during the mid-nineteenth century or to disclose the ignorance of life-saving techniques that were not discovered for decades is not the intent of the author. The intent is to acquaint the reader of travesties that took place during this time. The science and wisdom of medical care that we know now did not exist in 1860. Medical ignorance was a contributing cause of death for a vast number of people and is supported by substantial evidence.

Primary sources of disorganization, ignorance, and neglect in sanitation and medical care are highlighted in the ensuing pages. Conditions of disease are presented as a precursor to a discussion of the roots of disease. The fact that many of these diseases were preventable is underscored by the description of their causes. Finally, the implementation of existing knowledge by efforts to reform the medical system will also be reviewed.

Medical training did not follow a consistent or rigorous course. Essentially, anybody who had the money to buy a degree could become a doctor, and in many states, this degree, as easy as it was to acquire, was not required for one to practice medicine. It became widely apparent that through the unwise application of a laissez-faire philosophy toward the medical profession, and in response to a shortage of medical workers, Americans welcomed unrestricted competition at a time when diseases were running rampant. A physician's first experience with surgery was sometimes guided solely by a medical journal, and many doctors began practicing medicine without having ever closely observed an operation. One such individual was South Carolina's James Marion Sims, an excellent student from Jefferson Medical College who began his practice with only a set of surgical instruments, seven medical books, and a supply of medicine.[7]

Basically, the components were in place for a change in the health care establishment at the outset of the Civil War, but medicine was in no shape to meet this eventual emergency. Oliver Wendell Holmes totally agreed with this when he published his famous declaration, "I firmly believe that if the whole 'materia medica,' as now used, could be sunk to the bottom of the sea, it would be all the better for mankind, and all the worse for the fishes."[8]

Holmes, along with other noted individuals of the period, denigrated the concept of not only how inadequate the medical field was, but also the medicines being used to treat people. Holmes further argued that some young practitioners themselves undoubtedly felt that "the sick would be better off if they trusted entirely to nature rather than to the haphazard empiricism of the doctors, with their blistering, bleeding, and monumental dosing of medicine."[9]

Below-average opinion of doctors held by the public, which also pervaded the United States Army, was one of the factors responsible for the disorganization of the army's medical department when the Civil War broke out. Preparation for a contest of endurance did not seem necessary since public opinion on both sides held that the conflict would end quickly.

Subsequent to a long hiatus with little military action since the Mexican War, the medical department had essentially become soft. Most doctors had been to medical school and had served an apprenticeship at some point but, not surprisingly, they were unprepared for the rigors of war, especially in regard to gunshot wounds and the disease problems associated with masses of new soldiers crammed together in poor living conditions.

The United States Congress was also notoriously stingy in its allocation of funds to army medicine. General distrust of medicine played a major role in the parsimonious attitude from members of Congress toward the medical department. The Confederate Congress, however, budgeted much more money for medicine.[10] An additional hindrance attached to Union medicine was the long-standing inertia of the army medical department, as managed by Surgeon General Thomas Lawson, a veteran of the War of 1812. Lawson's sole concern "had always been to reduce his departmental budget—he considered medical books a waste of money."[11]

As a consequence of these situations, the medical department was unprepared for the massive mobilization of 1861. The number of army doctors had been low even before the first shot was fired on Fort Sumter. The Union Army had thirty surgeons and eighty-three assistant surgeons, charged with the care of fifteen thousand men. This small number of men found themselves to be the core of a medical department suddenly burdened with thousands of new recruits. During the year before the war, 111 surgeons had cared for 30,000 cases (roughly two illnesses per soldier per year). Of this group, only 138 died, which was mainly attributable to tuberculosis and gunshot wounds sustained from Indian fighting. Secession also brought with it the resignation of three surgeons and twenty-one assistant surgeons. After another three assistant surgeons were dismissed for disloyalty, the war began with ninety-eight officers in the Union Medical Department.[12]

Almost immediately when the Civil War began, the growth of combat far outpaced the rate of expansion of the medical corps. The lack of a decent transportation system or field hospital system left many wounded soldiers lying amid the dead for days, to be relieved from their anguish by fellow soldiers or by family members that came to retrieve them. Reliable ambulances were the exception more than the rule in the early years of the conflict.

The first ambulance was a two-wheeled wagon called the Coolidge Ambulance, named after surgeon Richard H. Coolidge, which was pulled by two horses. The second type, which was pulled by four horses, was a four-wheeled wagon called the Tripler Ambulance, named after surgeon Charles S. Tripler. The most prominent was a four-wheeled wagon pulled by two horses, which was called the Wheeling or Rosecrans Ambulance, named after General W.S. Rosecrans.[13]

When a wounded man found his way to a hospital, which happened with more frequency in the later years of the war, after ambulances and field hospitals became common fixtures, a soldier was still not safe in the care of a doctor because surgery was a risky undertaking. A wounded man's chances for recovery seemed to vary according to his injury.

Author Stuart Brooks points out that "35 percent of wounds involved the arms, 36 percent the legs, 18 percent the torso, and 11 percent the head."[14] According to official records, "49 percent of abdominal wounds, and 28 percent of all head and chest wounds were fatal. 90 percent of deep, penetrating wounds in the abdomen and head were fatal."[15] Brooks also emphasized that "wounds to arms and legs were not as deadly, but effectively removed a soldier from combat." Amputations were performed when a limb suffered a severe laceration or a compound fracture because attempts to repair smashed limbs usually ended in lethal infection. The site of the amputation determined a patient's chances for recovery. The farther a cut was made from the torso, the safer the patient was from the inevitable infection. Removal of a foot at the ankle had a 94 percent survival rate, while 17 percent of patients survived amputation of a leg at the hip.[16]

Surgery, as an art, was still young at the outbreak of the Civil War, since anesthesia had not been introduced until the late 1840s, and had limited utilization. Nineteenth-century surgeons had learned from experience what they could or could not do, and experience had taught them to stick with simple procedures. Three out of four Civil War operations were amputations because surgeons, wary of infection, rarely risked abdominal, thoracic, or head surgery. In general, surgery was most successful when an injured, wounded, or otherwise damaged body part was simply removed. Not only was the wound removed entirely, but also the surgeon had less contact with the interior of the patient. While many infections were unavoidable, many were directly caused by septic surgical practices. Brooks also noted that most surgeons "had no time for such effluvial manners—there was too much cutting to be done."[17]

The sheer magnitude of patients prevented the surgeons from being able to wash their hands or instruments until the end of the day. Dr. Keen, looking at the period in retrospect, noted:

> We operated with clean hands in the social sense, but they were undisinfected hands. We used undisinfected instruments from undisinfected plush lined cases, and still worse, we also used marine sponges, which had been used in prior pus cases, and had only been washed in tap water. If a sponge, or any other instrument fell on the floor, it was washed, squeezed in a basin of tap water, and used as if it were clean. The silk, with which we sewed up the wounds, was undisinfected. If there was any difficulty in threading the needle,

we moistened it with bacteria laden saliva, and rolled it between bacteria infected fingers.[18]

Due to military blockade shortages, Confederate surgeons even resorted to penknives and carpenter saws.[19] It is not surprising, then, that surgery on or near the trunk of the body was fatal—surgeons themselves were a primary cause of infection. Doctors and nurses lowered hospital mortality rates by the war's end with proper ventilation and greater cleanliness.

Army surgeons were representative of America's physicians, ranging from competent professionals to utter frauds. The amount of publicity drawn by incompetent doctors may be out of proportion to their numbers, but their prevalence was recognized even by 1860 standards. In other words, though they might have been poor surgeons, better doctors were not to be found.

Charges of incompetence were not unfounded. In an inspection of the surgeons of two hundred regiments, only 176 were qualified. Roughly one out of eight was described as being incompetent, negligent, and inept. One regiment's surgeon and assistant surgeon, a father-and-son team, affords a particularly bad example. The former had been a barber and an occasional cupper and leecher and had no medical degree. The son's medical education was also doubted. This was not surprising, though, since no medical board had ever examined them.[20]

In accompaniment with volunteer officers and soldiers, doctors were also recruited from private life after varying degrees of examination. These ranged from the rigid tests imposed on candidates to a careless weighing of merit by which the imperfectly qualified imposter has not been found wanting. The medical doctor in charge of surgery at a hospital would nominate a prospective surgeon, who was confirmed by the governor of the state with the approval of the examining board.[21]

Attitudes of doctors toward sick and wounded soldiers helped to foster their generally unflattering reputation. The trying conditions of the job wore down many a doctor's compassion for his patients. American novelist Louisa May Alcott, working in the Washington General Hospital, wrote that one surgeon "had acquired a somewhat trying habit of regarding a man and his wound as separate institutions, and seemed rather annoyed that the former should express any opinion on the latter, or claim any right in it while under his care."[22]

Alcott also pointed to his "way of twitching off a bandage, and giving a limb a comprehensive sort of clutch, which, though no doubt entirely scientific, was rather startling than soothing." One anecdote from her diary described Dr. P.'s expectation that his patient assist in his own treatment. "Here, my man, just hold it this way, while I look into it a bit," he said one day to Fritz G., putting a wounded arm into the keeping of a sound one and proceeding to poke about among the bone and visible muscles. Alcott observed, "The poor man passed out from the pain, at which point I continued to hold his wounded arm up for inspection."[23]

The sick rate in the Union army in 1861 was 3,882 cases per one thousand soldiers. The rate fell the following year to 2,983 per thousand and dropped further to 2,273 in the final year of the war. As a rule, black men suffered from greater sickness. While the average annual rate for whites was 2,435 per thousand, with 53 per thousand resulting in death, there were 3,299 cases of sickness reported for every one thousand black soldiers in Union regiments, with a death rate of 143 per thousand. Each white soldier, then, reported illness two and one-half times per year, while black soldiers, on average, would go to sick call three and one-third times annually. The death rate from disease was three times as high for blacks.[24]

Soldiers appearing on the sick list peaked around July and August. In October 1862, there was a second peak following a large influx of fresh recruits. The diseases to Civil War soldiers in the Deep South were at their worst in the heat of summer and in the early months of autumn. However, one could expect exposure to cold weather to increase disease rates in the winter months.

Problems experienced by soldiers, while characteristic of nineteenth-century warfare, had been less severe in the antebellum United States Army. For the year ending June 30, 1862, the mortality rate was twice that of the peacetime rate of the regular army during the eighteen years prior to 1860.[25] So devastating was disease that even if a unit saw no combat, its health life was only about one year. If no recruits were added, which was often the case; regiments were either discontinued or consolidated into other fighting units.[26]

Disease was a force to be reckoned with by military strategists as much as by individual men. No unit escaped its touch for the duration of the war, training was hindered, and extremely sick soldiers had to be withdrawn from the field to recover. Entire military companies could be rendered impotent. Several military campaigns were not renewed because of disease.[27]

Epidemics had greater influence on campaigns than on individual battles because of the longer duration and static periods. Dr. Paul Steiner noted that "sickness almost constantly burdened the military organization, and its harmful effects were commonly addictive to other adverse conditions." Steiner admits "the threat of disease according to season, geography, and experience of the troops...always had to be considered in military planning." In most cases, the Union and Confederacy had similar, if not equal, rates of disease. While there were campaigns and battles whose outcomes were decided by the sickness on one side or the other, losses to sickness felt by one side were usually proportionally equivalent to those felt by the other.[28]

Union and Confederate soldiers alike were tormented by a variety of illnesses. The biggest offenders were the same as in any war—typhoid fever, malaria, measles, pneumonia, mumps, dysentery, and diarrhea. Most diseases could be assigned to one of two general categories. Childhood maladies, true to their name, included sicknesses that were typically caught before puberty, and having had them once, a person was immune to subsequent attacks. The other grouping, camp diseases, was associated with the dirty living conditions and excessive crowding common to soldier camps and hospitals alike. Malaria, typhoid fever, dysentery, and diarrhea were the most hazardous members of this classification.

The spread of epidemic diseases, though chaotic in nature, followed a pattern. Childhood diseases struck susceptible soldiers immediately upon introduction to the crowded living conditions of camp life. Smallpox, varioloid (similar to smallpox), measles, scarlet fever, diphtheria, chicken pox, and mumps, among others, caused more damage when contracted in adulthood. Fortunately, not all were equally dangerous or prevalent. Smallpox, the deadliest of these infections, was so rare during the Civil War that Joseph Woodward, an assistant surgeon, did not include it in his 1863 study of camp diseases in the United States Army.[29]

Measles, the most common childhood disease, was not usually fatal by itself but was particularly troublesome because a bad case left soldiers vulnerable to deadly complications. It was the most destructive of the infantile diseases, and more damage was attributed to it in the first few months of the war than to any other cause. Because of the early onset of measles attacks, many men were struck while waiting to be mustered into the army.[30]

Although camp diseases usually struck soldiers after childhood diseases, malaria, typhoid fever, and dysentery did not become epidemic without the right seasonal environment and geographic factors. Statistically, the South, and especially the Deep South, proved unhealthier in this respect than the northern states, due to a generally warmer climate. The southern press proudly boasted in 1861 that the Union soldiers would not stand a chance against their destructive climate of disease.[31]

Medical authorities indicated that tendencies of diseases in temperate zones appeared to peak in the hottest weather and disappear after the winter frosts. It was also observed that the deltas and alluvial margins of great rivers, the borders of tropical streams, and regions of extensive marshes and swamps were the most volatile habitations of these maladies.[32]

Sanitary Commission Officer James Poole noted during an inspection, "There have been a few cases of intermittent fever found, three in one regiment is the largest number, as this camp was situated near a pond." Poole added, "Men who slept outside at night, to avoid the foul air of a sealed tent, were more prone to malarial fevers."[33] Examination of the causes of disease highlights how much the poor health of Civil War soldiers was the result of human error and how the rates of many diseases could have been lowered through greater attention to the mitigation of their causes.

More interesting than the course of the diseases and the damage they incurred are the factors that caused them. These factors included climate, neglect of sanitation, and poor nutrition. Disease was also made more prevalent by the practice of recruiting unhealthy men. In an inspection of Union forces in the Ohio and Mississippi Valleys in June of 1861, Sanitary Commission President H. H. Bellows, observed that the common complaints of soldiers on the sick list and in the hospital were "diarrhea, pneumonia, measles, and typhoid fever." Bellows declared, "It was obvious that the recruiting had been careless, and the men who were sick were mainly those who should never have been permitted to enter the service."[34]

Negligent inspections of new soldiers were due to the need for soldiers to fill an ever-increasing demand as the war escalated. Sick and old men turned out in high numbers in 1861 and 1862 because they wanted to fight. In the Confederacy, dire straits forced the passage of several Conscription Acts, which gradually increased the maximum and decreased the minimum ages of prospective soldiers. Many volunteered in answer to a patriotic call to duty, but unhealthy recruits were as much of a handicap to the war effort in the South as in the North.[35]

Environmental conditions—particularly the purity of water, quality of food, and cleanliness of soldiers and campsites—determined rates of disease in the army. The unbalanced diet soldiers were forced to endure was a serious menace to their health. While Union soldiers generally had enough to eat, as food was not commonly in short supply, the Confederates were forced to do without food more frequently, primarily because of supply problems.[36]

A majority of the responsibility for diseases in the soldier population can be ascribed to dietary deficiencies. Dr. W. H. Van Buren, inspecting volunteer camps in July of 1861 for the Sanitary Commission, reported, "There is not probably a single surgeon attached to a volunteer regiment in the vicinity of Washington, who will not testify that the troops are now suffering in health for want of vegetables." Van Buren also wrote, "Directly, or indirectly, diarrhea is, in almost every case, attributed to this cause." The inspector recommended that "the government keep a supply of vegetables with the army as it moved into the southern wilderness."[37]

Shortage of an adequate supply of pure drinking water was also a danger to soldiers, due to both organic and mineral impurities. Provisions were seldom made in the first year of the war for water supplies, and campsites were not always chosen with an emphasis on access to clean water. In another inspection of the units in the Ohio and Mississippi Valleys in the summer of 1861, Van Buren emphasized, "It is evident that change of water, and especially bad water, is the most immediate and serious cause of illness in all western camps at this time. Pains enough are not taken to place the camps with reference to the vicinity of good water."[38]

Unfortunately, in the nineteenth-century, the importance of sanitation was not commonly understood. In the early years of the Civil War, judging from the descriptions of personal cleanliness and camp hygiene, it might seem that the officers, doctors, and soldiers of the war had never even heard of soap. More likely, sanitation seemed to merely take a back seat to things that were more important, such as tactics and military training.

Short of keeping clean camps, constant movement seemed to be the best way to avoid health problems derived from living amid offal and excreta. An army that moved quickly seemed to benefit from leaving behind its waste, thereby contributing to an overall lessening of sickness. Sanitary Commission inspectors also reported that "when an army can shift its ground at will, danger to health ... can always be avoided by doing so."[39]

Countless military officers were amazed that soldiers who had lived their lives in at least minimal accordance with social graces could live like pigs in the army. The Confederate General Robert E. Lee was amazed by the personal grooming habits of soldiers who had once been functioning members of society. Bothered by the sickness, which he thought the soldiers encouraged through poor grooming, General Lee wrote, "They are worse than children, for the latter can be forced."[40] As was found, the soldiers did have to be forced. When camp policing improved, so did the overall health of the armies. Most of the blame for the unsanitary conditions during the first years of the war can be directed at the lax enforcement of discipline.

Disorganization plagued Union and Confederate forces in 1861. By the end of the war, the Union Army operated like a well-oiled machine, but it took considerable pushing to reach that point. One of the more important blunders of the first year was the general neglect of the danger of disease. Volunteer officers were usually engrossed in strategy and tactics; they did not concern themselves with camp discipline. It would be months before the officers finally understood that close attention to detail was not degrading and that a loose disciplinarian was an enemy rather than a friend of his men.[41]

In 1861 and 1862, nobody was more critical of the officers of the Union Army than the United States Sanitary Commission inspectors in their camps. Most of the inspectors indicated that:

> Union Military Officers generally take it for granted that their duty toward their men begins

and ends with drills, and parades, forgetting that camp disease is the most dangerous enemy they have to fear, and at the same time the only enemy against which vigilance and precaution are almost certain of success.[42]

The inspectors were constantly urged to encourage strict discipline. Many officers of the Sanitary Commission stressed the vital military importance of the strictest enforcement of proper hygiene as a necessity to the success of the Union cause.

Reputations of the buildings being used as hospitals were as bad as that of some military officers and doctors. This suspicion existed because hospitals were regarded as good places to avoid in the nineteenth century. Many Union soldiers thought that the hospitals were a good place to go to die. For many of the same reasons that camps were sources of disease, so too were hospitals. As with camps, they were at their worst in the beginning of the war. The quality of hospitals did not meet the needs of the rapidly expanding armies. Numerous buildings, which had formerly been hotels or large houses, were converted for this purpose. These buildings, though better than no shelter at all, were not always suited for their new function.

Hospitals in 1861, being invariably old structures, had been designed for some other purpose. The army had acquired these dilapidated buildings with low ceilings, small rooms, and only a few windows. Their design was not conducive to the ventilation necessary in patient wards. When the weather turned cold, hospitals lacking ventilation were forced to close their windows, thereby increasing the likelihood of epidemics. Many Sanitary Commission reports of hospitals in the Washington area noted a lack of proper ventilation. They were also surrounded by wet ground and usually suffered from poorly drained basements. Most of these reports stingingly noted "the cellars and above ground areas are damp, and undrained, and much of the wood work is actively decaying."[43]

Recognition of ventilation as a preventive measure against some diseases was a revolutionary idea; not that it was new, but rather that the American medical establishment was slow to see its merit. The education and reform of the medical service often fell to civilian organizations, such as the United States Sanitary Commission. The commission comprehended well that the cause of some of the diseases described thus far had something in common—they were preventable. Diseases could not have feasibly been eliminated from the Civil War, but the diligent work on the part of the Sanitary Commission lessened their virulence. It appeared that ignorance, with regard to disease, was clearly at fault for most of the suffering and death in both the Union and the Confederate forces.

Soldiers' aid societies dotted the landscape. In the North, their function was to send extra supplies where they were needed. While this was true of the South, their close proximity provided innumerable outlets for those with a desire to help in either patriotic or humanitarian ways.

Volunteer organizations existed mainly on the state level, but the United States Sanitary Commission was the only humanitarian aid society organized on a national level. It was able to effect systematic and operational change in aspects of army administration that pertained to the comfort of the soldier. Through admirable political zeal, it managed to implement a system of camp and hospital inspections, hand pick the surgeon general, and overhaul the structure of the Army Medical Bureau. Taking advantage of its connections in Congress and the upper echelons of the army, the Sanitary Commission was able to recognize, combat, and solve many of the disease-causing problems that were prevalent at the time.

The experience of Britain during the Crimean War (1854–1856) offered very powerful lessons that included insufficient preparation for hygiene. The British Sanitary Commission was eventually formed, and the United States Sanitary Commission was patterned after it. [44]

Britain's Sanitary Commission was invested with plenary powers to do anything which could improve the sanitary conditions of the troops, whether in the camps or in the hospitals. Author and historian Charles Stille wrote that "their work proved extraordinary, and thousands of deaths were prevented." [45]

The United States Sanitary Commission raised money through public and private campaigns. Funds were used for the employment of camp and hospital inspectors, along with hospital appliances not adequately supplied by the medical department.[46] These means helped the Sanitary Commission reach its basic goal of counteracting the neglect of sanitary precautions in camps and hospitals and to provide maintenance of the health and welfare of Union soldiers.

One of the most noteworthy achievements performed by the Sanitary Commission was its reorganization of the Army Medical Bureau, especially since the same resistance that nearly prevented the commission's formation had become a constant hindrance to its performance. The Medical Bureau not only made the Sanitary Commission's existence tenuous, but the bureau itself failed to provide adequate care for the soldier population.

Historian Drew Gilpin Faust, president of Harvard, indicated that leadership was needed in the Army Medical Bureau, and this reflected upon the reorganization of the Army Medical Bureau as a major contribution to the Union soldiers when she stated, "Yet for all the horrors of combat, soldiers dreaded dying of disease even more." She also observed that "death from illness or disease offered all of the evils of the battlefield, with none of its honors."[47]

Abraham Lincoln:
Leadership and Character Analysis

Leadership can be defined as an interactive conversation that pulls people toward becoming comfortable with the language of personal responsibility and commitment.

Leadership is a virtue that at times can be vague and ambiguous. Most everyone can learn to lead by discovering the power that lies within to make a difference and being prepared when the call to lead comes. Consequently, there is no set of defined rules for leaders to follow; there are only guidelines, perceptions, and ideas. To learn the art of leading, we definitely need role models such as Abraham Lincoln so that we can learn from their experiences and the stories they tell.

Due to Lincoln's honesty and integrity, his influence of people through the art of conversation and storytelling, and his ability to preach a vision and continually reaffirm it, we find that his character and conduct provide a solid basis on which to formulate our own leadership quests. Lincoln practiced what he preached.

Throughout his lifetime, he was subjected to a great amount of personal tragedy and professional misfortune; hence, he was fully aware of what it was to experience a downward spiral that seemed infinite. When he became president, he recalled this darkened period of his life.

Trust, honesty, and an exuded integrity were virtues that Lincoln shared with his followers with a personal touch. Scholarly evidence does show that leaders who are not hesitant to tell their subordinates the truth, even when the news is bad, gain greater respect and support for ideas than their less-virtuous counterparts.

Conversation was something Lincoln not only enjoyed but also thrived on to exchange views and ideas. This was one of his chief forms of persuasion. During his years of practicing law, he had to be able to express himself fluently, whether in an office setting or in a courtroom. Due not only to his innate ability to converse, but also his knack for story telling, the assumption could be made that one on one Lincoln could easily influence anyone of just about anything.

William Henry Herndon, a law partner and associate of Abraham Lincoln, declared, "Lincoln never poured out his soul to any mortal creature at any time, and was the most secretive—reticent—man that ever existed." Judge David Davis, who knew Lincoln for many years from his practice on the judicial circuit and served him as an adviser in Illinois politics, agreed wholeheartedly. Using nearly identical words, Davis insisted, "Lincoln was the most reticent—secretive man I ever saw—or expect to see." With considerable understatement, Lincoln himself conceded in 1861, "I am rather inclined to silence."[1]

The factual record of Lincoln's public activities is more complete after he moved to Springfield in 1837, but throughout his life, he carefully guarded his feelings and kept his personal affairs out of the public scrutiny. As a politician, Lincoln rarely revealed what he was thinking until he made up his mind, and in conversation often tested his ideas by arguing against positions he supported. Visitors quite frequently mistook his unpretentiousness for frankness, but as Republican senator Lyman Trumbull of Illinois noted, "He communicated no more of his own thoughts and purposes than he thought would subserve the ends he had in view."[2]

There are a number of qualities regarding Lincoln's character and personality that simply cannot be fully explained without resorting to some dubious psychological theory. Many of these include his burning ambition and desire to improve himself, his fear of intimacy and extraordinary private reserve, supported by his wife's assertion that he had trouble expressing what he felt most deeply, his estrangement from his father and family, his ability to draw other men to him while not being drawn to them, and the way he served as a father figure for a number of intensely admiring young men while he was a rather ineffective father himself. His personality seems paradoxical, well captured by the juxtaposition of his hearty sense of humor and his deep-seated melancholy.[3]

Abraham Lincoln was a fatalist. That, at least, was what he told many people over the course of his life. Lincoln informed his Illinois congressional ally Isaac Arnold, "I have all my life been a fatalist." Henry Clay Whitney, a Springfield law clerk, readily asserted, "Mr. Lincoln was a fatalist," and also stated, "He believed…that the universe is governed by one uniform, unbroken, primordial law."

William Herndon affirmed Lincoln "believed in predestination, foreordination, that all things were fixed, doomed one way, or the other, from which there was no appeal." Even Mary Todd Lincoln admittedly acknowledged that her husband had been guided by the conviction that "what is to be will be, and no cares of ours can arrest, or reverse the decree." What this meant in practical terms, as Herndon discovered, was that Lincoln believed "there was no freedom of the will, that men had no free choice."[4]

Confirming Lincoln's fatalism, Herndon referred to "his early Baptist training, a defective physical organization, and even on a sort of crude genetic determinism, based on what Lincoln suspected was the possibility of his mother's illegitimate birth."[5]

Motives, therefore, ruled human action, and they possessed that power because motives appealed at the most basic level to human self-interest. His idea, recalled Herndon, "was that all human actions were caused by motives, and at the bottom of these motives was self."

Lincoln evidently had little patience with the idea that human behavior could arise spontaneously from some inherent human goodness or even that it could be educated to guide its choices by some rule of other-worldliness, impartiality, or disinterested benevolence. Herndon quite often told the audiences during his controversial Springfield lectures in 1866 that Lincoln always expected "the snaky tongue of human selfishness to wag out."[6]

Herndon made unequivocal references to serious trouble in Lincoln's marriage; however, he inexplicably ignored evidence showing that Lincoln's married life was "a domestic hell on earth, a burning, scorching hell, as terrible as death, and as gloomy as the grave."[7]

Historian Allen C. Guelzo claimed "Lincoln's moods shielded his inner self from public inspection; behind the affability, there remained both the pervasive sense of melancholy, and a distinct reserve that not even his closest friends and protégés could dispel, or penetrate." With all his awkwardness of manner and utter disregard of social conventionalities that seemed to invite familiarity, there was something about Abraham Lincoln that enforced respect.

Journalist Donn Piatt wrote, "No man is presumed on the apparent invitation to be other than respectful." Piatt was told at Springfield that "this accompanied him through life." Among his associates, when young, he was a leader, looked up to, and obeyed because they "felt of his muscle, and his readiness in its use." Researcher and author Henry Clay Whitney also found that there was in Lincoln "an indefinable something that commanded respect. It was a respect that invited, and sometimes even indulged, treatment as an equal, or even a brother. That something also provided a curtain that the respectful found them unable, and unwilling to penetrate."[8]

Lincoln rallied with extreme difficulty and determination, even in the face of his own episodes of depression. According to author, essayist, and Lincoln researcher Joshua Wolf Shenk, Lincoln "developed diligence, and discipline, working for the sake of work, learning how to survive, and engage." Without the discipline of his middle years, he would not have had the fortitude to endure the disappointments that his great work entailed. Lincoln, as Shenk states, "was not just working, but doing the work he felt made to do, not only surviving, but also living for a vital purpose."[9] Shenk observed, "The struggle with depression was a continuing one, not one to be overcome but endured." He noted how Lincoln advised a grumbling general who felt humiliated at having only three thousand men under his command to "act well your part, and there all the honor lies. He who does something at the head of one regiment will eclipse him who does nothing at the head of a hundred."[10]

Shenk contended that "the overarching lesson of Lincoln's life is one of wholeness. Knowing that confidence, clarity, and joy are possible in life, it is easy to be impatient with fear, doubt, and sadness." Perhaps in the inspiration of Lincoln's eventual passing we can receive some of the fortitude and instruction about all it took for him to get there and all that it continues to take.[11] Shenk reasoned that "whatever greatness Lincoln achieved cannot be explained as a triumph over personal suffering. It must be accounted for as an outgrowth of the same system that produced it." This is not transformation, but integration. Lincoln did great work because he solved the problem of his melancholy. The problem of his melancholy, however, added more energy to do all his great work.[12]

Historian Doris Kearns Goodwin took a fresh approach to Lincoln by deciding to study in depth the men he appointed to his cabinet, among whom were his chief rivals for the Republican Party's presidential nomination in 1860. Goodwin thinks Lincoln can be understood and appreciated more fully by studying his interactions with those who were "better known, better educated, and more experienced in public life," such as Secretary of State William Henry Seward and Treasury Secretary Salmon P. Chase.[13]

Goodwin greatly admired Lincoln. She noted astutely that "he truly enjoyed a profound self confidence." She further argued that an "even-tempered disposition" enabled him to overcome a "melancholy temperament" and "function at a very high level," even in the face of "appalling pressures." Only someone with "remarkable talents" could transform an unstable collection of bruised egos into a team that could fight and win an enormous war.[14]

According to Goodwin, "Lincoln knew exactly what he was doing during the winter before the war started." He allowed the would-be compromiser Seward to make conciliatory overtures toward the disaffected South in hopes of preserving the peace, and he even incorporated many of Seward's words in his inaugural address. Lincoln also knew where to draw the line, and he "retained an astonishing degree of control over an increasingly chaotic, and potentially devastating, situation." While Seward seemed to age ten years in just a few months, Lincoln alone had the composure and that inner strength in order to make the right decisions.[15]

Historian Michael Burlingame charged that "Abraham Lincoln did not like women." His stepmother recalled that he "was not very fond of girls," a conclusion supported by his stepbrother, who said that "he did not take much interest with the girls because he was too busy studying." He also wrote that Mr. Lincoln's "attitude toward women in general was puzzling, especially his passivity in his dealings with them." [16] His kindness toward women appeared to be just as notable as his discomfort. Thomas P. Reep wrote:

> When he was called upon to survey the original town of Petersburg, Ill. in February, 1836, he found that Hemima Elmore, the widow of an old friend who had been a member of his company in the Black Hawk War, had bought a little tract of land within the grounds to be surveyed and had built a home where she lived with her children. If the streets of Petersburg were to run straight North and South, a part of her house would be in the street. Lincoln adjusted the street lines so they would miss the Elmore household. [17]

Historian James M. McPherson points out that "Lincoln, most emphatically did not think in abstractions, and rarely spoke in platitudes." McPherson stated that Lincoln's pre-eminent quality as a leader "was an ability to communicate the meaning, and purpose of the war in an intelligible, inspiring manner that helped to energize the people to make the sacrifices necessary for victory." [18]

J. T. Duryea of the United States Christian Commission emphasized, "In temper he was earnest, yet controlled, frank, yet sufficiently guarded, patient, yet energetic, forgiving, yet just to himself; generous yet firm." Duryea also believed "his conscience was the strongest element of his nature. His affections were tender, and warm. His whole nature was simple, and sincere—he was pure, and then was himself."[19]

Pennsylvania Republican leader Alexander K. McClure wrote, "I regard Lincoln as being very widely misunderstood as to one of the most important attributes of his character." Despite his friendliness, McClure observed, "It was not easy to get to know Mr. Lincoln." Even those who did professed not to understand him. Mr. Lincoln gave his confidence to "no man without reservation." He trusted many, but only within the carefully studied limitation of their usefulness, and when he trusted, he confided only to the extent necessary to make that trust available.

According to scholar Paul Angle, "he had as much faith in humankind as is common amongst men, and it was not because he was of a distrustful nature or because of any especially selfish attributes of his character. He thus limited his confidence in all his intercourse with men."[20]

Being an instinctively cautious person, Abraham Lincoln thought long and hard before acting or speaking. Author Rufus Rockwell Wilson claimed to have found a clue to Lincoln's hush-mouthed caution in the way he played chess—not boldly, but defensively, keeping his next move entirely to himself. Wilson emphasized that "while playing chess, Lincoln seemed to continually think of something else." Those who played with him suggested that "he played as if it were but a mechanical pastime to occupy his hands while his mind is busy with some other subject." Lincoln played what many chess players call a "soft game, rarely attacking." Wilson contends that he "let his opponent attack while he concentrated all his energies in the defense—awaiting the opportunity of dashing in at a weak point at the expenditure of his adversary's strength."[21]

Lincoln was just as slow to act. As Justice Department official Titian J. Coffey recalled, one of Mr. Lincoln's most amiable qualities was the patience and gentleness with which he would listen to people who thought they had wrongs to redress or claims to enforce. However, sometimes, when his patience had been abused for selfish or unworthy purposes, he was quite capable of administering a caustic rebuke in his own way.

His patience was remarkable, but it could be strained. When confronted by an army officer who complained about Lincoln's failure to rule favorably on his case, Lincoln retorted, "Sir, I give you fair warning never to show yourself in this room again. I can bear censure, but not insult."[22]

Lincoln contemporary Francis B. Carpenter declared:

> The great predominating elements of Mr. Lincoln's character were first, his great capacity, and power of reason; secondly, his excellent understanding; thirdly, an exalted idea of

the sense of right, and equity; and fourthly, his intense veneration of what was true, and good. [23]

According to William Herndon, "Mr. Lincoln possessed extraordinary empathy—the gift, or curse of putting himself in the place of another, to experience what they were feeling, to understand their motives, and desires." Herndon emphasized, "Lincoln believed that the great leading law of human nature is motive. At the bottom of these motives was self." He often defied me "to act without motive, and unselfishly, and when I did the act, and told him of it, he analyzed, and sifted it to the very last grain." Being an analyzer of the laws of human nature, "he could form no just construction of the motives of the particular individual. He knew little of the play of the features as seen in the human face divine. He could not distinguish between the paleness of anger, and the crimson tint of modesty, in determining what each play of the features indicated, as he was pitiably weak." [24] William Herndon also contended that:

> All the follies and wrongs Mr. Lincoln ever fell into, or committed, sprang out of these weak points; the want of intuitive judgment; the lack of quick, sagacious knowledge of the play, and meaning of men's features as written on the face; the want of the sense of propriety of things; his tenderness, and mercy; and lastly, his unsuspect-

ing nature. He was deeply and sincerely honest himself, and assumed that others were so. He never suspected men; and hence in dealing with them he was easily imposed upon. [25]

It was affirmed, according to Herndon, "that the great predominating elements of Mr. Lincoln's peculiar character were his great capacity and power of reason; his conscience, and his excellent understanding; an exalted idea of the sense of right, and equity; his intense veneration of the true, and the good."

Herndon felt that Lincoln was cautious, patient, and enduring; he had concentration and continuity of thought and profound analytical power. His pursuit of truth was indefatigable. In the grand review of his peculiar characteristics, nothing creates such an impressive effect as his love of the truth. His life is proof of the assertion that "he never yielded in his fundamental conception of truth to any man for any end." Lincoln reasoned from well-chosen principles with such clearness, force, and directness that the tallest intellects in the land bowed to him.

Herndon stated that "the office of reason is to determine the truth. Truth is more or less the power of reason, and Lincoln loved truth for its own sake. It was to him reason's food." [26]

White House aide William O. Stoddard noted that "among the daily applicants for an interview with the President were representatives of every class and grade in the social scale, and every corner of our glorious Republic." Yet, it would be hard to deny that, "he was perfectly at home with any, and all of them." Lincoln "professed the utmost respect with men whose superior culture and information he frankly acknowledged, or for whose moral dignity or great achievements they possessed." Stoddard also believed:

> Self-possession is sometimes the consequence of overwhelming self-esteem, or an ever-present consciousness of the possession of power. With Lincoln, it was more or less the result of his utter absence of self-consciousness. His thoughts rarely reverted to any impression, which he might be making, and he was graceful, at least easy, and natural. [27]

According to author William Lee Miller, Lincoln aides John G. Nicolay and John
Hay both agreed that:

> His judgment outran the average mind. While others fretted at things that were, his inner consciousness was abroad in the wide realm of possibilities, busily searching out the dim, and difficult path towards things to be. His natural attention to ordinary occupations affords no indication of the double mental process, which was habitual with him. [28]

The well-known agnostic Robert G. Ingersoll insisted that "Lincoln was an immense personality—firm, but not overly obstinate. He influenced others without much effort, and they submitted to him as men submit to nature. He was severe with himself, and lenient with others, almost ashamed of tenderness."

Ingersoll felt that "Lincoln said and did the noblest words and deeds with that charming confusion—that awkwardness—that is the perfect grace of modesty."[29]

Cornelius Cole, who was elected as a Union Republican to the Thirty-eighth Congress (March 4, 1863-March 3, 1865), observed, "His deportment never missed, because it was the expression of his friendly feeling for all. He did not offend because he felt no animosity for anyone." Always in consultation, "he was argumentative, but not dictatorial." Cole judged him to be a listener open to conviction, yet if his own reasons were well founded and no one had a better reason to offer, he could not be moved. Cole added, "He was never offensively opinionated."[30]

Psychologist, writer, and Lincoln researcher C. A. Tripp stated that "Lincoln always had a tendency to react very sharply to death; he never seemed to accept it, and this sharp reaction to death was but one more of his many routes into severe depression." He endured death throughout his life. His brother, Thomas, died when Lincoln was three years old. His mother, Nancy, died when he was nine years old. Sarah, his sister, died in childbirth when he was nineteen years old. Sons

Edward and Willie died in childhood. Informed of the death of Colonel Elmer Ellsworth, a personal friend and the first officer casualty of the Civil War, Lincoln "sobbed profusely not only at the time and with official visitors standing close by, but also days and months later, often in public, and sometimes at the mere mention of Elmer Ellsworth's name." According to Tripp, Lincoln also had a strong reaction as to "what happens to the body of a friend or loved one as water seeps into the grave."[31]

Abraham Lincoln regarded simplicity and logic as the foundations of communication. He appeared to be more interested in persuading his listeners with facts and logic than impressing them.

Springfield attorney Charles Zane observed:

> Intelligent men with impartial and liberal minds, while listening to Lincoln's arguments, appeared to want to agree with him. He never awakened prejudice by narrow and uncharitable statements or inferences. He never unnecessarily irritated his adversaries. While he did not arouse the passions of the "hurrah boys" as much as some other speakers, his influence was greater with thinking men.[32]

Lincoln had many distinguishing traits before he became president, but these grew in importance during his tenure. Without question, his life was subjected to periods of melancholy. He was a believer in the doctrine of fatalism and was somewhat superstitious. He was seen as a homely man, careless of his looks, plain looking and plain acting. Lincoln held his moral and professional views with the same inflexibility with which he held his political views, but he could be persuaded when his convictions were in conflict with each other, which included army deserters.

Estimates of the number of deserters range well over one hundred thousand, but Lincoln saw a need for clemency. "He pardoned a considerable number of Union soldiers in a conscious effort to boost morale of northern forces," wrote historian Bell Irwin Wiley. According to one anecdote, Lincoln said:

> They are the cases that you call by that long title cowardice in the face of the enemy, but I call them, for short, my leg cases. However, I put it to you, and I leave it for you to decide for yourself. If almighty God gives a man a cowardly pair of legs, how can he help their running away with him?[33]

Union soldiers admired Lincoln because of the perception that he took an interest in their well-being. In 1864, Lincoln ordered the War Department to commute the death sentences of deserters to confinement until the end of the war and to allow commanding generals to reinstate convicted deserters if it was thought that they would be of use to the service.[34] Sixty-two deserters who were to be executed were spared in a single act in May 1864.[35] Lincoln assented to very few death sentences imposed by military courts and only after he had examined the facts and determined that the sentence was appropriate.

Lincoln's case-by-case approach and sparing of lives met with some objections.

Leniency could provoke the officers who were in charge of the soldiers. Colonel Theodore Lyman, for instance, attributed the lack of military discipline to uncertainty about the death penalty and the "false merciful policy" of the president.[36]

When Lincoln first took office, quite a few of his colleagues and most ardent adversaries had taken the position that he would be a malleable president. Edward Bates, the attorney general, wrote in 1861 that "the president's an excellent man, and in the main, wise, but he somehow lacks will, and purpose, and, I greatly fear, he has not the power to command." Historian Jan Morris observed that:

> To sum up his character I should say that he had greater natural mental calibre than any man I ever knew. He was extremely just and fair-minded. He was unquestionably ambitious for official distinction, but he only desired a place to enable him to do good and serve his country and

kind. He was an artful man, and yet his art had all the appearance of simple mindedness.[37]

Morris indicated that "as the years went by, Lincoln's strength became apparent to all. It was not a rocklike strength." Morris contended, "He remained essentially flexible in his thinking, like a tough bit of rope, which might swing from side to side, but would never break." Those who perceived this recognized the possibility that Lincoln could be talked into almost any concession of interest.[38]

Cordelia Harvey:
Nineteenth-century Humanitarian

Cordelia Harvey is someone who most definitely deserves a place of respect among the women of the nineteenth-century whom the Civil War brought to the fore as leaders. These leaders included a number of extremely prominent individuals such as Dorothea Dix, Anna Dickinson, Clara Barton, and Louisa Mae Alcott. In some respects, Cordelia could also be classed as a prominent national figure. One of the many significant humanitarians of her time, she achieved renown as a sanitary agent for the United States Sanitary Commission.

She could justifiably be compared to Florence Nightingale, who was conceivably one of the most extraordinary nurses in history. Nightingale was the superintendent of nurses for British soldiers during the Crimean War (1854–1856).[1] Although not a nurse, Cordelia became directly involved with the American Civil War. These extraordinary women shared the same fundamental outlook. They both dedicated their lives to the sick, the oppressed, and the suffering.

Once President Abraham Lincoln issued the proclamation for soldiers in 1861, Wisconsin women rallied to support the Union during the Civil War; these women became nurses, hospital matrons, sanitary agents, and ministers. Many were forced to cope with the extremely rigorous hardships of supporting their families without a male counterpart.

Writing about Cordelia, two contemporary observers, L.P. Brockett and Mary C. Vaughn, noted that "to a lady who had seen nothing of military life, of course, all was strange." The experiment she was making was, they said, "one in which very many kind-hearted women have utterly failed—rushing to hospitals from the impulse of a tender sympathy, only to make themselves obnoxious to the surgeons by their impertinent zeal, and by their inexperience and indiscretion, useless and sometimes detrimental to the patients." Brockett and Vaughn also went on to say:

> With the wisdom that marked her course throughout, she basically comprehended the delicacy of the situation, and was not long in perceiving what she could best do, and wherein she could accomplish the most good. The facility with which she brought, not only her own best powers, but the influence universally accorded to her position, to bear for the benefit of the suf-

fering soldiers, is subject of remark and wonder among all who have witnessed her labors.[2]

Author William D. Love described Cordelia Harvey as "a woman with a fine sense of humor, a fund of homely common sense, and a deep religious feeling, which expressed itself in feelings rather than deeds." In short, he suggested that "she was an extremely human, lovable person, of the highest type of womanhood, unselfish, unconsciously great; someone that Wisconsin can be proud of having the honor to claim as its daughter."[3]

Nineteenth-Century Women

In nineteenth-century America, the role women would play in society began to change dramatically. This was the beginning of a whole new world for women, and America in general. Many of these women began to realize that there were opportunities for them outside of the home and that they could have a place in the world as well as the men. It was a time when the feminist view was being born and traditional views of women were changing.

Women took their part in working to help slaves gain their freedom in the anti-slavery movement. They also felt that they could identify with the way slaves were being treated, and therefore wanted to help them. Many middle-class women began to realize that they were equal to men and wanted to be treated in the same way and partake in similar activities. This included obtaining an education, working, and being able to support themselves without the help of men.

Writer, teacher, and outspoken feminist Margaret Fuller observed that this nineteenth-century woman:

> Learn the lighter family duties, while she acquires a limited acquaintance with the realm of literature and science that will enable her to superintend the instruction of children in their earliest years, with no faculties capable of eternal growth and infinite improvement, we would still demand for her a far wider and more generous culture, than is proposed by those who so anxiously define her sphere.[4]

Fuller also stated, "The 1840s were a decade of reform in which individuals identified themselves in part by their attitudes toward reform itself." Americans were reexamining the principles of democracy and individualism. Although women could undertake humanitarian reforms and maintain social respectability, Fuller contended that "direct political involvement (such as lobbying) and public political argumentation was still very risky." Fuller truly admired the risk takers and praised them every chance that she had. She "implicitly identified herself with them and their public work, displaying a redefinition of self as woman."[5]

Traditional roles of women in society were changing, and their role in the family was changing also. With women wanting the right to vote, work, and go to school, middle-class life as they knew it would be drastically changed. Women no longer wanted to be in the home with the children, cooking and cleaning; they wanted to get out into the world. There was still an extremely long way to go before women were to be accepted in society, and this was just the beginning.

Socially, the nineteenth century can be defined as a time characteristic of working husbands coming home to perfect homemakers, loving children, and dinner cooking on the stove. This displays the habitual lifestyle that almost all families of this time modeled because it was the mold that society created. It was understood that true womanhood was the centerpiece of the nineteenth-century female identity.[6]

Adhering to these values, women, then, were expected to find unlimited happiness and security in their marriages. By conforming to these nineteenth-century societal expectations, women and men alike learned to cling to their roles. Women were expected to follow these four main virtues: piety, purity, submissiveness, and domesticity.[7]

True womanhood foreshadowed a view of womanhood to come. An ornament to society is true to history. Women generally grew tired of their role as true women and desired to play a more creative role in society. True womanhood was just one phase in the defining of womanhood. As society continues to invent numerous molds that promote conformity, however, each role aids womanhood in becoming a desired ideal position in society.[8]

As for women in American society, a number of changes were forthcoming. Women played very important roles in religious and social reform movements, such as missions, societies, abolition, and the temperance movement. Many asserted themselves by speaking out publicly before mixed audiences and seeking leadership positions in the movements, thereby violating criticism by overstepping the boundaries of masculinity. This made these outspoken women ever more conscious of their inferior status and ever more dedicated to the pursuit of their rights.

Doris G. Yoakam, author and woman's rights activist who was the first to identify the relationship between the dominance of the woman's sphere ideology and cultural constraint on nineteenth-century women's rhetorical opportunities, called the mid-nineteenth century an "age of experimentation," and claimed that "almost anything could happen—even public speaking by women."[9] Oratory, the act of speaking in public on civic matters, remained a male prerogative in the United States until the early 1840s, when increasing numbers of women began ignoring the taboo and established a female oratorical tradition.

Historian Kenneth Cmiel quotes William Lloyd Garrison, the nation's leading radical abolitionist, defending the right of women to speak in public by declaring, "We allow our women liberty of the press—why should we deny them liberty of speech?"[10]

Cmiel emphasized that "in one sense, this issue was resolved by the 1850s, when the number of female orators expanded considerably." By the end of the decade, at least in the North and West, it was established that women could speak in public. However, the issue was not completely closed until after 1860. "For one thing, Southern women did not begin to speak in public until the Civil War," Kenneth Cmiel said.[11]

Reflecting on Cordelia's Early Years

Cordelia Harvey was born on December 7, 1824 in Barre, New York, and was the daughter of John and Mary Perrine. In the mid-1840s, the family moved to Southport (now Kenosha, Wisconsin), where she taught school and eventually married another teacher, Louis Powell Harvey, in 1847. Louis, who was born in East Haddam, Connecticut, was largely self-taught. He served both as a tutor and teacher at the Southport Academy. In 1843, he became the managing editor of the Southport American, a weekly Whig newspaper. The Harvey's had one daughter, Mary, who died in infancy. Cordelia's early life did not differ from that of other Wisconsin women of her day who spent their lives in small towns, busy with their daily routines.[12]

According to Virginia Penney, author and teacher who devoted herself to enlarging the industrial sphere of women, stated, "There were very few professions that women could enter in the nineteenth-century. Medicine and law required an education to which women often did not have access." She stated that "teaching, especially primary school children, was considered very appropriate for young single women." Despite the numerous opportunities for women to teach in public schools, there was very little training available. "Often merely completing the eighth grade was considered sufficient training for teaching," she said.[13]

Margaret Fuller, journalist, critic, and woman's rights activist associated with the American transcendental movement, stated, "One of the noblest professions is that of a teacher who requires superiority in tact, quickness of sympathy, gentleness, patience, and a clear and animated manner in narration, or description." To be a good teacher, Fuller said, one must have "sincere modesty combined with firmness, liberal views with a power and will to liberalize them still further, a good method, and habits of exact investigation."[14]

After departing Kenosha in 1850, the Harveys settled in Shopiere, Wisconsin. In 1859, Louis Powell Harvey was elected secretary of state. Due to Harvey's strong personality and political sagacity, he was elected governor of Wisconsin in 1861 and assumed his office in January of 1862. From the day of the firing on Fort Sumter, Louis and Cordelia began work for the soldiers and the families. In April, 1862, Governor Harvey, while visiting the Wisconsin troops in Tennessee after the battle of Shiloh, was about to pass from one boat to another, fell overboard, and drowned in the Tennessee River.

The Demise of Governor Louis Harvey
The Chicago Daily Tribune carried this article on April 26, 1862.

> The night was pitch dark, and the rain was falling. The boat (the steamer Dunleith) that Governor Harvey and his party expected to embark from was near the one they were to board (the Minnehaha). The Governor walked out on to the guards (walkway) at the stern of the boat. The guards were not more than two or three feet from the water, and entirely unprotected by any railing, and from some cause, which must forever remain a mystery, but probably under the impression that a railing was there, the Governor paused not in his step, until he fell struggling in the water. Dr. Wilson, of Beloit, and Dr. Clark, of Racine, were near him when he fell, and heard his cry for help. Dr. Wilson extended his cane, which was grasped, but dragged from his hands by the weight. Dr. Clark swung himself into the water from the stern of the boat, grasping the stern wheel, in the hope that the Governor might lay hold of his person, as he swept past. However,

it was all in vain. The waters demanded their victim, and would not release him. With struggles and subdued cries, the body swept past the boat, and disappeared under a barge near it in the stream, only to be recovered some days later.[15]

Governor Louis Harvey, after completing his compassionate work of mercy in the spirit in which he commenced it and having attained all the success that could possibly have been hoped for, was on his return home. It was a cruel accident, which thus arrested his homeward steps.

Being one of Wisconsin's most prominent leaders during the Civil War, Cordelia took up her late husband's mission to improve the healthcare of many wounded Union soldiers. Her husband's successor, Lieutenant Governor Edward Salomon, was then asked to appoint her as the state's sanitary agent. Judge Timothy O. Howe, taking her case to the acting governor, emphasized that:

> Mrs. Harvey is visiting us. You can imagine something how she suffers from the loss of her husband. Her friends desire that she should find employment with which to occupy her mind. However, what employment can a woman find? She is urged to try a school for young ladies, but she fears the derangement of the times will forbid success, and so do I. She has thought of a hospital, but you know General Hammond is

taking them under his own care exclusively, and her strength will not warrant her in contracting for day labor. This morning I suggested to her the idea of being appointed allotment commissioner in place of Mr. Holton. It pleases her. It is a kind of missionary labor, to which she is fully equal, and in which she will be, I am confident, very successful. I know of no one more energetic than she is in whatever interests her. You know how deeply she has interested herself in the welfare of the army. She could plead the cause of a soldier's family to the soldier himself, I think, with great effect.[16]

Governor Edward Salomon eventually named Cordelia as a sanitary agent in September 1862.

Cordelia's Leadership Qualities

What manner of woman was Cordelia Harvey? From all accounts, she was not beautiful. Although she possessed a strong magnetic personality and was delightfully frank, she also had charming manners. Her tact was unusual, allowing her to succeed in accomplishing what she set out to do. United with this tact were an indomitable will and an untiring persistence.

With these traits, it might be imagined that she lacked tenderness and sympathy. Such was not the case, however. It has been recorded that her motherly heart and sympathetic nature caused many of the soldiers to call her the "Wisconsin Angel."[17] United with these qualities of character and temperament was her experience in social affairs; she knew how to approach the highest official as well as the humblest private.

Nevertheless, she had a fine sense of humor, a fund of homely common sense, and an extremely deep religious feeling that expressed itself in deeds rather than in words. She was unquestionably modest and very often said that every patriotic woman in Wisconsin deserved as much praise as she. She was truly unselfish and unconsciously great.[18]

Even though she was a leader, she had to be persistent and use persuasive tactics in order to convince President Abraham Lincoln what she felt was best for the Union soldiers, namely building hospitals in the North, primarily in Wisconsin.

Harvey seemed to have an ability to influence others to follow her. Decisions had to be made very quickly while she was visiting the various camps and hospitals. As sanitary agent, she had that authority to get things accomplished. When authority was not recognized, she would write to Wisconsin Governor Salomon and ask him to use his influence. This usually resulted in getting the proper care and supplies to the soldiers. She was able to influence others to help her in her quest of caring for the soldiers. She was very seldom turned down because her efforts were of utmost importance.

Openness and honesty were among her strong suits. She did not give false promises just to make her case. Her goal was to show that a choice was in the best interest of everyone concerned. She used neither coercion nor force to persuade, but gentle kindness.

The War Years

Stories regarding the role of women in the Civil War have often been romanticized. They are often portrayed as spies and abolitionists, sharply cut patterns that most certainly do not fit the average woman and her contributions to her cause. During the war, women were put into many diverse situations. There was not one war experience, but rather a time when women were placed in extraordinary circumstances. Women at this time used their traditional roles and the tasks associated with them to support the army and sent packages to help make their men on the front more comfortable.

Cordelia Harvey effectively used her elevated position as the wife of a governor, her patriotic sense of duty, and her traditional care-giving nature to exceptional heights.

A large part of the Wisconsin home-front war effort was that of the organized groups that women set up just after the war began, not only to provide solidarity among those left behind in the difficult times of war, but also to make goods to be sent to their loved ones located on the field of battle. They were also an instrumental help in healthcare, as they provided supplies for the ever-crowded and budget-strapped field hospitals, worked as nurses, and raised money for the hospitals. It was the combined effort of both Mrs. Harvey and the women throughout the state of Wisconsin that allowed them to play an integral role in aiding the health and well-being of soldiers in the field and the dependents they left behind while significantly altering the ways Union soldiers were cared for while injured on the battlefront.

After sending their young men off to war, many women next went to work providing supplies so that their men would be comfortable while they were away. These groups soon became recognized nationally as Soldiers' Aid Societies, and they had countless affiliates of various names throughout the Northern states. The Wisconsin Soldiers' Aid Society was formed soon after the first Civil War battle at Bull Run/Manassas, Virginia. [19] There were 229 reported associates in the Wisconsin branch, while the headquarters was located in Milwaukee. [20]

The service the Soldiers' Aid Societies provided was one of immeasurable benefit. They helped the government untangle some of the red tape that was associated with paying the salaries of soldiers, and in turn, getting those payments into the hands that needed it: the women at home struggling to raise children without a father. It was estimated shortly after the war that the material contributions of the Wisconsin Soldiers' Aid Society alone was nearly six thousand packages sent to the field and with a monetary value of nearly two hundred thousand dollars.[21] The Wisconsin branch was celebrated for their work, and the national headquarters repeatedly complimented them for their zeal and efficiency.[22] The group was instrumental in terms of morale; in reminding the soldiers that the women back at home remained ever loyal to the cause for which they were risking their lives.

They went about the work that would put soldiers' minds at ease about the loved ones they had left behind and allow them to concentrate fully on the task at hand: to end the war in favor of the Union Army and its commander-in-chief, President Lincoln.

The United States Sanitary Commission was created shortly after President Lincoln issued his first call for seventy-five thousand troops in April 1861. Women throughout various parts of the country banded together to confer on how best to serve the soldiers. Regardless of creed or social position, women at once began to form a national organization to minister to the army.[23]

Lincoln vigorously snubbed this idea at first and basically described it as a "fifth wheel to a coach," but then, finally, along with Simon Cameron, Secretary of War, gave in on June 18, 1861, by establishing an order authorizing the formation of the United States Sanitary Commission.[24]

There was fervor for the Union cause around the state, but the contributions of Cordelia Harvey were of a different sort. She was not involved in the manufacture of clothing and supplies for the soldiers. She came from a different social strata; it was not every woman who was the wife of a governor that had visited field hospitals and would eventually have an audience with the president.

Harvey evaluated the field hospitals and persistently fought to change conditions and send wounded soldiers north to recover from their wounds and illness, even going so far as to have a series of private meetings with the president. The efforts of both Cordelia and the women throughout the state of Wisconsin played an integral role in aiding the health and well-being of soldiers, while altering the ways they were cared for while injured on the battlefront. They also helped the dependents of soldiers left behind.

Cordelia was stationed at many hospitals, being directly in charge of evaluating conditions and reporting back to the government agencies. She judged the conditions and also how effectively the supplies were moving. In general, sanitary agents like Harvey were the eyes and ears of the government as a nonmilitary presence in the hospitals.

She quickly went about her work, traveling to St. Louis, visiting all the area hospitals. Cordelia soon became a popular figure among the wards, but shortly after her arrival, Harvey, overtired and exposed to contagion, became ill and was forced to go north in order to recover.[25] Cordelia found most of the field hospitals lacking the proper facilities to be able to care for the Union soldiers, and she used her illness as proof, by concluding that:

> It would be beneficial if soldiers were sent North to recover rather than left to languish in the field hospitals where contagious diseases, and the hopeless atmosphere caused soldiers to grow despondent, and their conditions to worsen. I was sick among them last spring, surrounded by every comfort, with the best of care, and although I was determined to get well, I grew weaker, day by day, until, not being under military law my friends brought me North. I recovered entirely, simply by breathing northern air.[26]

Historian Gillian Gill asserted that in retrospect, Florence Nightingale was concerned with these very same issues. According to Gill, Miss Nightingale stated, "The problem as I see it, lay in the army's failure to protect its men against disease, and to promote their recovery once they fell sick."[27]

Gill emphasized that Florence was extremely vehement in her convictions when she reasoned that "a healthy man who breathed bad air, drank impure water, and was unable to keep his body clean tended to fall ill, and if that man was surrounded by thousands of others living in the same conditions, his illness was easily passed on to others if they were not moved to other locations."[28]

The thought of sending soldiers north was always rejected right from the beginning, due to the fear that it would increase the rates of desertion.[29] Cordelia was never discouraged and regularly wrote to Wisconsin Governor Salomon describing how men in quite poor condition were often discharged, citing the adverse effects of the warm weather until hope, courage, and finally life itself failed them.[30]

She concluded most of her letters with the idea that was quickly becoming the focus of her position, which revolved around the necessity of northern hospitals.[31] With a strong feeling that northern hospitals would benefit the army, Harvey suggested, "If you let the sick come north, you will have ten well men in the army one year from today, where you have one well one now, whereas if you do not let them come north, you will not have one from the ten, they will all be dead.[32]

Harvey wrote to Governor Salomon whenever she had situations that required immediate attention. It was not always easy to express herself or to use the right language when describing the conditions that she was witnessing both in the camps and in the various field hospitals. The situation she was part of was made more complicated by the fact that she had no formal training as a nurse and was not knowledgeable of the situations she encountered.

Drew Gilpin Faust, eminent historian and an expert on the Civil War and the American South, wrote about Union surgeons, women nurses, and relief workers and how they witnessed a similar sense of verbal incapacity. It was truly a struggle at times to get thoughts together in order to be able to write something coherent about what was taking place. Faust continues this thought when she talks about Cordelia Harvey writing home from Tennessee to Madison's Wisconsin State Journal saying, "There are times when the meaning of words seems to fade away; so does our language fail to express the reality. A fact I never fully realized as when attempting to depict the suffering, both mental, and physical, which I have witnessed within the last ten days. [33]

Faust also wrote about how Kate Cumming, a southern author, had somewhat similar thoughts regarding the horrific scenes that she encountered. She reacted to her entry into the various hospital wards, saying, "I do not think that words are in our vocabulary expressive enough to present to the mind the realities of that sad scene. The suffering far exceeded language and understanding. [34]

The South had been generally recognized for diseases such as malaria and fevers that would ravage a body unaccustomed to life in that climate. Many of the camps that Harvey visited were alongside the various rivers throughout the southern countryside, promoting a damp environment and hindering the recuperation for the sick and wounded soldiers.[35]

Included in her assumption regarding the benefits of the soldiers recovering in the North were multitudes of grateful women in many of the northern cities who worked tirelessly for the soldiers. They showed this with their determined efforts in sending packages to the army with the goods that were needed to maintain and improve the soldiers' health.

Cordelia regularly asked governors of many of the other states to meet with President Lincoln and talk up the idea of making northern hospitals a priority. This was requested so that the wounded men might be transferred north, to the respective hospitals in their own states, where they would be nearer their friends and family.[36]

Harvey had to overcome a number of very serious concerns from not only Lincoln, but also from the Union generals in the field about the soldiers abandoning their place in the army simply by being put in too close of a proximity to their homes and families. She had to be able to justify her reasoning for moving the soldiers north by explaining the eventual rewards that would be gained if this mission were accomplished.

Harvey's Campaign Strategy for the Union Soldiers

In September 1863, Cordelia Harvey advanced on the White House to argue and remonstrate with President Lincoln about his war. President Lincoln met this courageous, patriotic woman head-on. He spoke with her day after day for a number of days. During this dialogue process, Lincoln demonstrated an exquisite mindfulness; all the while he was making a ruthless inquiry into his very own personal motives.

Cordelia faced opposition in her quest to transfer the wounded soldiers to northern hospitals. She said, "The necessity for establishing military hospitals in the North had been a subject of much thought among our people, but it was steadily opposed by the authorities."[1]

Eventually, Governor Edward Salomon wrote to President Lincoln to make northern hospitals a priority so the wounded men might be transferred to their own home states, where they would be nearer their friends and family. He even referenced the fact that Cordelia Harvey had recuperated fully by breathing northern air after her bout with contagion.[2]

Cordelia had to learn about effective persuasion strategies. Realizing the needs of the president and knowing the heavy burden that was placed upon his shoulders, she had to be able to justify her requests so that a mutual understanding could be reached. She had to convince him that he would share the eventual joy in preserving the well-being of the Union soldiers.

The medical officers in charge of the camps were also not in favor of northern hospitals. Many of them tried to keep Cordelia from getting too involved, saying, "She had better stay away; the air is full of contagion, and contagion and sympathy do not go well together."[3]

Author Judith E. Harper stated, "Even Dorothea Dix, Superintendent of Female Nurses, had conflicts with surgeons and medical officers from the very beginning." Harper related, "The physicians wanted total control of the hospitals, the nurses, and all other aspects of patient care. They seemingly thought they knew more of what the soldiers needed then the nurses and volunteers."[4]

Requests for discharges or transfers to other hospitals were frequently turned down. One young officer, Captain Jameson, who happened to be a medical officer at Helena, told Harvey, "The general feeling here is that it was much cheaper for the government to keep her sick soldiers in hospitals on the river than to release them elsewhere."[5] Cordelia's reply informed him that many individuals believed it:

> To be their duty to keep these sick men alive as long as possible. To be sure, their uneaten rations increased the hospital fund, and so enabled your surgeons to generously provide all needed delicacies for the sick, but the soldiers drew the pay from the government all the same. Don't you think, sir, it would be a trifle more economical to send these poor fellows North for a few weeks, to regain their strength that they might return at once to active service.[6]

Harvey spoke to William Sanger, one of the Sanitary Commission workers, asking why no one did anything to discharge or transfer the men. He replied that "surgeon's signatures were often overruled by the director with a disapproval marked over them." Sanger said, "When the soldiers went in person to see the director about the matter, they were severely reproved, and ordered back to the hospitals. Many of them never returned, for brokenhearted, they...laid down by the roadside, and died."[7]

Cordelia, seeing these conditions firsthand, became even more determined to fight for northern hospitals. She felt the idea to be "so natural that we never once thought the authorities would oppose the movement. For nearly a year this question was agitated... but all in vain."[8]

Although many people were in favor of the northern hospitals, it was largely a matter of convincing the government and army officials that the idea would be more of a benefit than a headache.

These men had signed their freedom away to serve their nation's cause, only to be injured in the process and eventually be sent to a government-sponsored hospital near the battlefield upon which they had fallen. Cordelia described the hospitals as "mere sheds filled with cots as thick as they could stand with scarcely room enough for one person to pass between them."[9] Receiving various accounts of crowded conditions in the hospitals along with the disease, lack of supplies, and the inspections, Harvey came to the conclusion that, "We are pained to say that these places are uncleanly, uncomfortable, unhealthy, and a disgrace to our soldiers."[10]

Disease was ever present, and this was at a time before any of the medical technologies of the modern age were in use. Amputations with a swig of liquor and a bullet to bite, reusing dirty bandages, surgeons operating without washing between surgeries—it was a nightmare for healthcare, and a soldier hoped that he would not have to go to one of these havens of disease.

Rarely would a soldier be able to avoid going to the field hospital for one reason or another. It was inevitable that at some point during that drawn-out struggle one would succumb to either disease or a wound. Men were used as assistants in the hospitals if it became necessary, often used to bury the dead.[11] Some of the field hospitals were close to the camps themselves so that it would not take much for a whole area to be taken by an epidemic of disease.

There was no doubt that the simple act of separating the diseased from the healthy would have been a great service done to those still able to fight. The only obstacle in the way was the government, which saw this practice of transferring soldiers as an impediment to the war effort since it took men from the field, where they were needed. The president, along with his advisors, felt that there would be armies without enough men to fight, and if a few of the soldiers had to be sacrificed in the name of the greater good, it was a sad but acceptable loss for a just cause.

The only option she had was to take the argument to all of those who opposed it. Cordelia Harvey then decided to take her case to the only man who had the power to implement a national policy of transferring soldiers north to heal. Her task would not be easily won; she was going right to the man who had ended northern furloughs in the first place, fearing desertion of the soldiers.

Cordelia admired the president, not only as a human being, but also because he was a leader during such a traumatic time. Given her apparent temperament to believe in other people and that she admired those in leadership positions, it stood to reason that if she admired the president, he should also look favorably toward her. Harvey struggled with this dilemma during her meetings with Lincoln. She did not waver, but followed what her instincts led her to do and eventually succeeded in having President Lincoln relent in his opposition to northern hospitals.

The Lincoln/Harvey Debates

Cordelia Harvey eventually gained admittance to the White House, not only because of her position as a former governor's wife and United States Sanitary Commission Sanitary Agent, but also through the recommendations of Governor Salomon and Senator Doolittle.[12]

For a year this question was urged with all the force that logic, position, and influence could bring to bear, but all in vain. Despairing of any other route to success, Harvey went to Washington and stated:

> I entered the White House, not with fear, and trembling, but strong and self-possessed, fully conscious of the righteousness of my mission. I was received without delay. I had never seen Lincoln before. He was alone, in a medium sized

office-like room, no elegance surrounded him, and there was no elegance in him. He was plainly clad in a suit of black that ill fit him. At his side stood a high writing desk and table combined; plain straw matting covered the floor; a few stuffed chairs and sofa covered with green worsted completed the chamber of the president.[13]

President Lincoln's first comment after listening to the purpose of Cordelia's visit was that "he had thought the issue of northern hospitals had already been settled, and wondered what else remained to be discussed." She plainly stated to him, "Many soldiers... must have northern air, or die. There are thousands of graves all along our southern rivers, and in the swamps, for which the government is responsible, ignorantly, undoubtedly, but this ignorance must not continue."[14]

Cordelia, being a virtuous woman, was clearly overstepping her bounds, for at that time she was addressing the president of the United States and accusing him, although indirectly, of having a hand in the deaths of thousands of Union soldiers. Lincoln was still concerned with the rates of desertion, but Harvey assured him that "dead men cannot fight and they may not desert."[15] She also reminded the president of the loyalty of his soldiers and the patriotic duty that they were performing by putting their lives on the line.[16]

This face-to-face meeting with the president would be her only hope, and she either needed to convince him or resolve that there would never be a northern military convalescence hospital. Lincoln then relayed to her the actual number of men that the government was paying in the Army of the Potomac in the eastern theater of the war, compared to the total number of men who were actually fighting in the Battle of Antietam. It turned out that there were only 83,000 men fighting, out of the 170,000 that were being paid.[17]

Lincoln was quite adamantly opposed to the idea of distant hospitals. He believed that the war might have been ended at Antietam and so implied that "if men had not been scattered across the North on furloughs for one reason or another, they would have been in the army where they were severely needed." Cordelia rebutted, "Since these men were not in northern hospitals, and since they did not exist, the example he gave was not a reason against having the hospitals."[18]

Appearing rather flustered by this response, Lincoln sent her to the secretary of war, Edwin Stanton, to discuss the matter with him. He informed the secretary "he should seriously listen to what she had to say."[19] This eventual meeting did not produce the positive results that Harvey had been hoping for. Stanton also explained that his position would be based upon what the surgeon general, already on a tour of battlefield hospitals reported, regarding the feasibility of northern hospitals and their benefits.

Cordelia was not satisfied because she knew that these inspections always had the same result: a continuation of the status quo, which led to more soldiers in field hospitals and the additions of many gravesites alongside the hospital perimeters. She told Stanton, "The medical authorities know the heads of departments do not wish hospitals established so far from army lines, and report accordingly."[20]

Having still not accomplished her goal, Harvey left the secretary of war and once again returned to President Lincoln. He received her yet again and expressed his exhaustion in hearing of the issue of the northern hospitals. Cordelia passionately pleaded her case by saying she was there to protect his strong reputation among the people "who may grow discouraged at the sight of so many friends dying when with appropriate health care they might recover, and once again serve their country loyally."[21]

Perhaps sensing that this might be her last chance to convince the president, she pleaded passionately for those soldiers that "were the first to hasten to the support of this government, who helped to place you where you are, because they trusted you. Men who have done all they could."[22]

She then went on to tell him that "she, unlike many that prepared reports about the hospitals, did not seek a higher appointment or any fame, but only to help the men she saw dying every day in hospitals."[23] She told him about the inspectors who would tour the hospitals and when they finally went into the fresh air, "took a deep breath as though they had just escaped suffocation, yet still reported in favor of that same hospital."²⁴

Her pleas were generally that of a sentimental nature and would invariably seem to have had a definite effect on any person, especially one who knew firsthand the difficulties facing the armies in a conflict that would test the entire nation for four long years. Harvey's final appeal to the president was that she had visited the regimental and general hospitals on the Mississippi River, from Quincy to Vicksburg, and sadly stated, "I come to you from the cots of men who have died, who might have lived had you permitted. This is hard to say but it is none the less true."²⁵

Cordelia's persuasive task had definitely proved to be extraordinarily difficult because, as Lincoln initially stated on her visit to the White House, "Madam, this matter of northern hospitals has been talked of a great deal, and I thought that it was already settled, but it seems not."²⁶

Harvey seemed to be able to encourage the tempo of her message even in the face of major differences of opinions and extremely strong emotions from Lincoln. This audience with the president had been a long, drawn-out, tiring affair that required numerous visits to the White House.

Frustration occurred during one meeting with Lincoln when Cordelia related that when she became ill and went north to recuperate, her feelings were that "the majority of soldiers sick and dying in the South would live, and be strong men again if they could be sent North."[27] Lincoln's reply was, "You seem to know more than I do."[28]

Feeling emotionally upset by the president's remark, she thought that the tears would come but was eventually able to gain her composure and then rallied when she finally said to him:

> You must pardon me, Mr. President, I intend no disrespect, but it is because of this knowledge, which I do know that you do not know, is why I come to you. If you knew what I do, and had not ordered what I ask for, I should know that an appeal to you would be in vain; but I believe the people have not trusted you for naught. The question is if you believe me, or not. If you believe me, you will give me hospitals, if not, well..."[29]

Lincoln's unsympathetic answer to this response was, "You assume to know more than the surgeons do."[30] Cordelia's response was:

> Oh no! Mr. Lincoln, I could not perform an amputation nearly as well as some of them do; I do not think I could do it at all. However, this is true—I do not come here for your favor, I am not an aspirant for any type of military honor. While it would be the pride of my life to be able to win your utmost respect, and confidence, still,

this I can waive for the time being. The medical authorities know as well as I do that you are opposed to establishing northern hospitals, and they report to please you, and desire your favor.[31]

After tirelessly listening to all of this dialogue from Cordelia Harvey, Lincoln caustically stated:

That I come from no casual tour of inspection, passing rapidly through the general hospitals, in the principal cities on the river, with a cigar in my mouth, and a rattan in my hand, talking to the surgeon in charge of the price of cotton, and abusing the generals in our army for not knowing, and performing their duty better, and finally coming into the open air, with a long drawn breath as though just having escaped suffocation, and complacently saying, "You have a fine hospital here; the boys seem to be doing very well, a little more attention to ventilation is perhaps desirable.[32]

Harvey, seemingly irritated by what President Lincoln had said, simply replied, "It is not thus."[33] She then went on to say, "I have visited the hospitals from early morning until late at night sometimes. I have visited the regimental, and general hospitals on the Mississippi River from Quincy to Vicksburg, and I come to you from the cots of men who have died, who might have lived had you permitted. This is hard to say, but it is nonetheless true."

Her message was a hard sell to the president. Cordelia recalled that as she spoke, "Mr. Lincoln's brow had become very much contracted, and a severe scowl had settled over his whole face. He sharply asked me how many men Wisconsin had in the field, that is how many did she send?" I replied, "About 50,000. I think; I do not know exactly."[34] Lincoln commented, "That means she has about 20,000 now." He looked at me and said, "You need not look so sober, they are not all dead."[35] She did not reply but noticed "the veins in his face filling full within a few moments, and one vein across his forehead was as large as my little finger, and it gave him a frightful look." She then indicated that soon, with a quick, impatient movement of his whole frame, he said, "I have a good mind to dismiss every man from the service, and have no more trouble with them!"[36]

A sense of hostility had begun to materialize. Lincoln seemed to be beside himself and apparently wanted to humiliate her in hopes that she would back down. She stated, "I was totally surprised at his lack of self-control, and I knew he did not mean one word of what he said, but what would come next? As I looked at him, I was extremely troubled, fearing I had said something wrong. He was very pale."[37]

During this heated exchange, she reluctantly indicated that the silence was extremely painful and said to him as quietly as she could:

> They have been faithful to the government; they have been faithful to you; they will be loyal to the government, do what you will with them; but if you will grant my petition, you will be glad as long as you live. The prayers of many grateful hearts will give you strength in the hour of trial, and strong, and willing arms will return to fight your battles.[38]

President Lincoln then bowed his head and, with a look of sadness that Cordelia would never forget, said, "I shall never be glad any more. The spell must be broken." She then said, "Do not speak so, for you will have so much more reason to rejoice when the government is restored, as it will be." Lincoln responded with, "I know, I know," while placing a hand on each side and bowing his head forward. He replied, "But the springs of life are wearing away." She then asked if he felt that his great cares were injuring his health. He responded, "No, not directly, perhaps."[39]

Harvey certainly kept trying to look for a way that she could influence the president. Even during their conversation, she would confront him if he seemed downtrodden and try to uplift him. As the conversation progressed, Lincoln commented on the fact that he thought the issue of northern hospitals was settled. She, on the other hand, intimated that it was not, and that is why she was there. She seemingly was, by her very nature, a person of great intestinal fortitude. Her comments were on the hospitals and more specifically, focused on the death and dying aspect.

Once again, her comments were, "Many soldiers in our Western Army on the Mississippi River must have northern air, or die. Thousands of graves lie along many of the southern rivers and swamps, and if you permit these men to come North, you will have ten men where you have one now."[40]

Lincoln could not see the force or logic in this argument. He said, "If your reasoning is correct it would be a good argument. I do not see how sending one sick man North is going to give us in a year, ten well ones."[41]

Cordelia countered with:

> Mr. Lincoln, you understand me, I think. I intended to say, if you will let the sick come North, you will have ten well men in the army one year from today, where you have one well one now; whereas, if you do not let them come North, you will not have one from the ten, for they will all be dead.[42]

Cordelia said he then responded with, "Yes, yes, I understand you; but if they are sent North, they will desert: where then is the difference."[43] She countered by saying that "dead men cannot fight, and they will not desert."[44] Lincoln retorted, "A fine way, a fine way to decimate the army, we should never get a man of them back, not one, not one."[45]

The major premise of this argument relates to Cordelia indicating to Lincoln the horrendous conditions of the camps and hospitals she had just finished visiting. He indicated that he had just visited these facilities and found them to be in relatively good shape. He did say in regard to the hospitals when talking to the surgeon in charge, "You have a very fine hospital here; the boys seem to be doing very well, a little more attention to ventilation is perhaps desirable."[46] Cordelia's effort in trying to convince the president what she wanted did not sit well with him. Initially and for quite some time after that, he would not have any part of it. It was only after a number of visits she had with him that he finally consented.

Cordelia described this on her final visit with Lincoln as he came forward, rubbing his hands and saying, "My dear madam, I am very sorry to have kept you waiting. We have but this moment adjourned."[47] Harvey replied, "My waiting is no matter, but you must be very tired, and we will not talk any more." He said, "No, sit down," placed himself in a chair beside her, and said, "Mrs. Harvey, I only wish to tell you that an order equivalent to granting a hospital in your state has been issued nearly twenty-four hours ago."

Cordelia indicated that she could not speak; she was so entirely unprepared for it and wept for joy. "I could not help it." When she could speak, she said, "God bless you, I thank you in the name of thousands of soldiers who will bless you for the act."[48] After, she said, "Do you mean, really and truly, that we are going to have a hospital now?" President Lincoln, with a look full of humanity and benevolence, finally said, "I do most certainly hope so." Harvey indicated that he spoke very emphatically, and no reference was made to any of his previously held opposition. "He said he wished me to come and see him in the morning and he would give me a copy of the order."[49]

Harvey's arguments had been powerful and passionate. Her dynamism, and more importantly, her firsthand knowledge of the situation in the camps and hospitals, presumably had an effect on Lincoln.

Cordelia finally realized that President Lincoln was definitely in command. All of the responsibility of war, however, weighed heavily on him. The demands were incessant, and almost unbearable. The decisions that Lincoln made were generally his own, and the correspondence on them was usually in his own hand. The ghosts of thousands of soldiers haunted him, along with tears of all their mothers and widows and children.

The Realization of Harvey's Success

Cordelia won Lincoln over as she deftly balanced the tone of urgency with a rhythm of patience and expressed the essence of a woman who understood just how to be heard. Her efforts were rewarded when President Lincoln signed an agreement for three military hospitals to be established in Wisconsin. When he offered to name the main hospital in Madison after Mrs. Harvey, she quickly declined, remembering why she was doing the duty in the first place, and asked that it be named in honor of her husband. Therefore, it was named the Harvey United States Army General Hospital.[50]

Eventually succeeding with her confrontation with Lincoln, Cordelia was present when the Harvey Hospital was established in Madison. The hospital was not intended to be used for the critically wounded or those with any major debilitating diseases, but rather as a convalescence hospital for the wounded men who could withstand the journey to a northern hospital.[51]

A lifesaving theory that she had used on the president regarding northern hospitals was soon proven true when one hundred men at the Fort Pickering hospital in Memphis, Tennessee, originally given the prognosis of nearly hopeless, were then moved to northern hospitals. Of this group, only seven died and five were discharged, as all the rest were returned to active duty.[52]

Cordelia seemingly had a remarkable insight or intuition to see that many soldiers' lives could be saved because of what she was attempting to accomplish in her meetings with the president. As was the case, the Union Army eventually became the beneficiary of this cause when it was continually reinforced with soldiers from the hospitals during the later years of the Civil War.

Lincoln distinguished himself as a public speaker. As Kenneth Cmiel stated, "Men like Abraham Lincoln mixed together high and low language to fit their needs. Their speech was at times refined, but at other times crude. They were often eloquent, but they were also often folksy." Nineteenth-century debates over language pitted those trying to accommodate the new styles of popular rhetoric against those who resisted.[53] Harvey may have never considered herself in that capacity. She was resolute, even bordering on the imperious. Cmiel has pointed out that "to be an orator, then, was to be a certain kind of person. It implied an ethos, a character that pervaded one's whole self." He also argued that "one literally could not be an orator without moral wisdom. For the true orator, virtue was a necessity."[54]

Cordelia's character was certainly in accord with this description. She, however, did not underestimate the worth of true womanhood by attempting to act in a distinctively manly way. Her experience as a sanitary agent gave her firsthand knowledge of what was transpiring on the battlefront and in the hospitals. Her charm seemed to be only surpassed by her personal and intellectual strength. These qualities allowed her to talk to the president in such a way as to not only get her message across to him, but also to indicate how good he would feel when all was said and done. The welfare of the Union soldiers seemed to intensify more and more with every breath she took and every word she spoke. The main thrust of her dialogue with the president was to share all of the details that she herself had witnessed while performing her task as a sanitary agent.

Cordelia Harvey's firsthand knowledge of the deaths of the soldiers in a hostile climate and an atrocious medical situation were definitely contributing factors in making the president relent.

Conclusion:
Theoretical Analysis

How did Cordelia Harvey change President Lincoln's opinion of northern hospitals? She used arguments that appealed to both his logic and sense of compassion. Lincoln's melancholy and his extreme hatred for death had also made him susceptible to her appeals. Although women were usually expected to remain in the background, Margaret Fuller argued, "The immortal being of women should not be deprived of its nature to grow as an intellect to discern as a soul to live freely and unimpeded; to unfold such powers as were given by the creator.[1]

Cordelia's opportunity to evaluate the hospitals was extraordinary, as was her chance to gain an audience with the president. She saw the need of the soldiers in the hospitals and camps, came up with a feasible solution, and then, using her persuasive tactics, fought for her idea at every opportunity. She basically relied on Lincoln's morality, but more importantly, on his hatred for death. Her arguments shed light on the serious conditions she had witnessed and the graves she had seen along the rivers and swamps. Still not convinced, Lincoln attempted to make her the secretary of war's problem but was eventually won over by her earnest perseverance.

Emotion is a common component in persuasion. In Harvey's situation, persuasion was achieved by the speaker's personal character. Her message was spoken so as to make it sound credible. People who are credible are believed more readily than others. A person's character may be the most effective means of persuasion he or she possesses.

The book Crucial Conversations: Tools for Talking When Stakes are High, states that "the first principle of dialogue should begin within your own heart."[2] The authors contend, "Skilled people start with heart, and begin their conversations with the right motives, and they stay focused no matter what happens."[3] Cordelia had the right motives and stayed focused. During her conversations with Lincoln she sensed hostility toward her and stated that she "was surprised at his lack of self-control, but knew he did not mean one word of what he said. Although, when I looked at him, I was troubled, fearing I had said something wrong. He was very pale."[4]

Kelly Patterson, management coach and leadership trainer, notes, "Now what? At this point, we may want to back off. If we push too hard, we violate both purpose and respect." Cordelia was aware of Lincoln's lack of self-control, but she also thought that maybe she was at fault. Patterson related that "rather than trying to get to the source of the other persons emotions, we either gracefully attempt to exit, or ask what he or she wants to see happen. In other words, encouragement."[5] While this dialogue was taking place, Lincoln became emotional regarding what she was requesting. The president bowed his head and, with a look of sadness, said, "I shall never be glad any more, the spell must be broken." Harvey then retorted with, "Do not speak so, you will have so much more reason to rejoice when the government is restored."[6]

Psychologist Robert B. Cialdini asserted that "a well known principle of human behavior says that when we ask someone to do us a favor we will be more successful if we provide a reason. People simply like to not only have reasons, but that the outcome of the favor will provide positive results."[7] Cialdini also pointed out "consistency (being adamant in your pursuit) does reap rewards. Inconsistency is an undesirable trait. The person whose beliefs, words, and deeds do not match their arguments, is viewed as indecisive, and confused. A high degree of consistency is normally associated with personal, and intellectual strength."[8] Cordelia seemed to be a person with enormous energy and extreme confidence in what she was attempting to do.

Harry Mills, chief executive of the international consulting and training company The Mills Group, stated, "If you sound energetic, and confident, you will then be viewed as energetic and confident. If you sound weak or timid, you will probably be seen as weak or timid. If you sound shrill and strident, people will treat you that way. Your voice can reveal how relaxed or tense you are, and also how tired you are; it can even indicate your emotional state."[9]

Paul Simon, one of the youngest elected state legislators in Illinois history (at 26 he was only a year older than Abraham Lincoln had been when he entered the state legislature), noted, "Lincoln had a high pitched, penetrating and not too pleasant of a voice."[10] Mills pointed out that "people tend to judge one another directly through sight, and hearing, and treat you accordingly."[11] Lincoln, being energetic and confident, was a great orator. His message was more important than the pitch of his voice. Cordelia Harvey was not an orator but was energetic and confident. The sound of her voice is not known, nor is it important, because as in Lincoln's case, the sound of the voice was not as important as the message she delivered.

Authors Maxwell and Dickman contend, "Passion is one of the most important elements of persuasion. It is the fire in your belly that makes you want to tell the story, which makes everyone want to listen. It is the why of the story—why you are telling it, and why we are listening to it."[12] Cordelia certainly had an abundance of passion.

Persuasive techniques take many shapes and forms. Robert V. Levine, professor of psychology at California State University, Fresno, believes that "authority generates respect, but a type of trustworthiness is even more compelling: that resulting from character." He stated, "Because moral trustworthiness is perceived as relatively unwavering, a little of it goes along way. Once a reputation is established, it grows legs of its own."[13]

It can be assumed that there was no doubt in the mind of President Lincoln of Harvey's moral trustworthiness and unwavering contribution she put forth as sanitary agent. Her attitude was above reproach, and her moral character and reputation certainly became widely known.

Attitudes based on issues should persist longer than attitudes based on simple cues. Professor Timothy Brock, of the department of psychology at the Ohio State University, agreed that "reflecting on one's thought process can have an impact on attitude strength whether attitudes have actually changed, or not." He stated, "If the message a recipient receives contains weak, and strong arguments, the recipient is able to resist." He then stated that "the recipient who resists has an impact on their confidence in their unchanged attitude until a stronger message is received, credibility and sticking to the facts is of utmost importance."[14]

In persuasion, credibility of sources is a prominent factor in trying to change someone's mind. Herbert

W. Simons, professor of communication at Temple University in Philadelphia, asserts, "The major determinants of source credibility are perceived expertise and trustworthiness." These include qualities such as "perceived intelligence, honesty and dependability, along with maturity and good judgment." Being able to use "power and dynamism" are of utmost importance. Simons relates, "Power is the extent to how the speaker is perceived by the audience in the give and take scenario, dynamism then includes verve, passion, enthusiasm, and above all, dialogue."[15]

G. Tarcan Kumkale and Dolores Albarracın of the department of psychology at the University of Florida, Gainesville, Florida, confirm, "Persuasive messages are often accompanied by information that induces suspicions of invalidity." They added, "Over time, however, recipients of an otherwise influential message may recall the message, but not the non-credible source. They become more persuaded by the message at that time, than they were immediately following the communication that followed up this commentary."[16]

Harvard psychologist Howard Gardner advances the view that there are seven, what he calls "levers," that are effective in influencing a person to change their mind: "reason, research, resonance, redescriptions, resources, rewards, real-world events, and resistances."[17] Gardner stated, "To those who deem themselves to be educated, the use of reason figures heavily in matters of belief. A rational approach involves identifying relevant factors, weighing each in turn, and making an overall assessment."[18]

Cordelia concluded very succinctly in her meeting with Lincoln that ill soldiers would recuperate better when moved to northern hospitals. Lincoln's thought process was that the soldiers who left the battlefront would desert and never return.

Gardner contends, "Research complements the use of argument by collecting all of the relevant data."[19] The data Harvey had collected was through her visits to the camps and hospitals. Cordelia had visited the various areas and had seen the atrocities taking place. She lived and breathed with the soldiers, eventually succumbing to illness with them. The president also stated that he too had visited these same areas and found them to be in very good shape.

Resonance occurs when something feels right to an individual and seems to fit the current situation. "The resonance concept denotes a view, idea, or perspective."[20] In Cordelia Harvey's case, having fallen ill herself from one of the camp diseases and eventually recuperating in northern air, she believed that what she was requesting was the right thing to do. Lincoln refused to accept this fact for fear that the soldiers would desert if they were placed in their own home areas. He maintained that they were better off near where the conflict was taking place. In fact, he was so adamant about this that he even cancelled furloughs so the soldiers would be there when needed. Cordelia vehemently disagreed with the reasoning of the president by stating that "dead men cannot fight, and they will not desert."[21]

"Representational redescriptions take different forms such as linguistic, numerical, or graphic to reinforce the message," states Gardner.[22] Harvey's message encompassed all of these traits, primarily the numerical and graphic. In the numerical realm, she indicated how many graves she had seen along the rivers because of lack of concern by the government and the graphic details of what she saw in the camps and the hospitals. She also reiterated, "If you will let the sick come North, you will have ten well men in the army one year from today where you have one now; whereas, if you do not let them come North, you will not have one from the ten, for they will all be dead."[23]

Author Gardner believes "the resources, and rewards factor indicates that the possibility for changing someone's mind tends to lie basically within the grasp of any individual whose mind is receptive to change."[24] This level comes into play when Cordelia makes reference to the fact that if the soldiers are sent north to recuperate, they will "give you (Lincoln) strength in the hour of trial, and strong and willing arms will return to fight your battles."[25]

Gardner writes, "Real-world news events in the broad scope affects many individuals, not just those who are contemplating a mind change. Included in this would be wars, and the availability of medical treatments that prevent illness, or lengthen life."[26] The use of news stories about the war bolsters one's perspective and can be used to effectively change minds. Harvey was able to do just that as the press exploited the travesties, as she so aptly described them.

Resistance is generally the most difficult lever of persuasion to overcome. Barriers to changing one's mind are created by age. Gardner says, "As people get older, their neural pathways are less susceptible to alteration." Gardner noted, "The emotions that a topic creates, and the public stand one has previously taken on a topic also play a key role."[27] Cordelia had to overcome these barriers because Lincoln was adamant in his decision of not allowing any movement of the soldiers. This proved to be a major turning point in order to overcome the president's resistance.

Lincoln scholar Harold Holzer said that the famous speech Lincoln delivered at the Cooper Union in New York on February 27, 1860, "was meant to be an antislavery lecture, and capped by a ringing warning to would be secessionists in the South."[28] He contended the speech reaches its climax by saying, "Let us have faith that right makes might, and in that faith, let us, to the end, dare to do our duty as we understand it."[29] Holzer asserts the speech "propelled Lincoln toward the Republican nomination, and to the presidency."[30] The speech carried the hopes and thoughts of the people about how to overcome slavery and is powerfully persuasive regarding moral issues as well. It ends with a request that the people do what is right for their country.

Cordelia was trying to do her duty for the country as she understood it. Her faith, passion, and moral duty to help the soldiers was the right thing to do. Having had the opportunity to visit with President Lincoln, she could speak with the authority of firsthand observation and the recognition of a need to be rational and human, even in the midst of a devastating Civil War.

Cordelia Harvey's Accomplishments

Following the opening of the Harvey Hospital at Madison in 1863, two other Wisconsin hospitals were opened, one in Milwaukee and the other one in Prairie du Chien.[31] Harvey's compassionate efforts had been reinforced when Dr. William A. Hammond, the army surgeon general, issued a policy that "authorized a transfer of all wounded and disabled soldiers unfit for duty for sixty days of convalescence."[32]

As the soldiers recuperated and were discharged, Cordelia, seeing the numerous orphans as a reminder of the war, transformed the Harvey Hospital into the Soldiers' Orphans' Home.[33] Although the Orphans' Home only lasted until 1875, it remained as another mark in the long list of extraordinary accomplishments.[34] Cordelia Harvey died on Feb 27, 1895.

Although raising a family alone was a difficult and foreign task for women at this time, it could also be seen as liberating. Women were out of their element, and yet they succeeded in organizing and making a difference in the war effort. They served an important function in maintaining the Union Army, both in terms of morale and supplies. Soldiers' Aid Societies provided women with a support system. While men bonded in the army as comrades in arms, women also bonded in a new way—as friends, as heads of households, and as essential components to the war effort. Wisconsin women shared a common cause, but there were different points of service. Soldiers' Aid Societies were the basic line of contribution. They provided the fundamental needs for the army, while in comparison; Mrs. Cordelia Harvey occupied an atypical position. Her opportunity as an evaluator for the hospitals was extraordinary, as was her chance to gain an audience with the president. She saw the need of the soldiers in the field hospitals, came up with a feasible solution, and then fought for her idea at every opportunity. Although Mrs. Harvey's recollections were dissimilar from the average experience of a Wisconsin woman during the Civil War, she remains no less relevant. Cordelia Harvey shared a similar experience, albeit at another level. She used her gender role as a caring, nurturing woman to generate change and make a difference in the way soldiers received treatment.

Although Lincoln had an aversion to women, his opinion changed when he realized the impact that women such as Cordelia Harvey made on the health and welfare of the Civil War soldiers. He acknowledged this debt of gratitude in Washington D.C. in 1864, by saying:

> I have never studied the art of paying compliments to women; but I must say that if all that has been said by many orators, and poets since the creation of the world, in praise of women, were applied to the women of America, it would not do them justice for their conduct during this war. I will close by saying, God bless all the women of America![35]

Bibliography

Adams, George Worthington. Doctors in Blue: The Medical History of the Union Army in the Civil War. New York: Henry Schumann, 1952.

Alcott, Louisa May. Hospital Sketches, Camp, and Fireside Stories. Boston: Roberts Brothers, 1869.

Angle, Paul M. Ed, Abraham Lincoln by Some Men who Knew Him. Chicago: Ayer Co, 1950.

Arnold, Isaac. The Life of Abraham Lincoln 1884. Lincoln: University of Nebraska Press, 1994.

Basler, Roy P., ed., The Collected Works of Abraham Lincoln. New Brunswick, NJ: Rutgers University Press, 1958.

Billings, John D. Hardtack and Coffee: The Unwritten Story of Army Life. Edited by Richard Harwell, Chicago: The Lakeside Press, R.R. Donnelly and Sons Publishing Co.1960.

Brock, Timothy C., and Melanie Colette Green. Persuasion: Psychological Insights and Perspectives. Thousand Oaks, CA: Sage Publications Inc. 2005.

Brockett, L. P., and Mary C. Vaughn. Woman's Work in the Civil War: A Record of Heroism, Patriotism and Patience. Philadelphia: Zeigler, McCurdy & Co., 1867.

Brooks, Stewart M. Civil War Medicine. Springfield, IL: Charles C. Thomas, Publisher, 1966.

Burlingame, Michael. The Inner World of Abraham Lincoln. Chicago: University of Illinois Press, 1994.

Carpenter, Francis B. Six Months at the White House with Abraham Lincoln. New York: Hurd and Houghton Publishing, 1867.

Chittenden, L.E., Personal Reminiscences: Including Lincoln and Others 1840–1890 New York: Richmond, Croscup and Company, 1893).

Cialdini, Robert B. Influence: The Psychology of Persuasion. New York: Morrow and Co. 2000.

Cmiel, Kenneth. Democratic Eloquence: The Fight over Popular Speech in Nineteenth-Century America. New York: William Morrow and Company, Inc., 1990.

Cumming Kate, Journal of a Confederate Nurse (Baton Rouge: Louisiana State University Press, 1959).

Cunningham, H.H. Doctors in Gray. Baton Rouge: Louisiana State University Press, 1958.

Doster, William E. Lincoln and Episodes of the Civil War. New York: G. P. Putnam, 1915.

Duffy, John. The Healers: The Rise of the Medical Establishment. New York: McGraw-Hill Book Company, 1976.

Faust, Drew Gilpin. This Republic Of Suffering: Death and the American Civil War. New York: Alfred A. Knopf, 2008.

Field, Maunsell B. Memories of Many Men and Some Women. New York: Harpers, 1874.

Fuller, S. Margaret. Women in The Nineteenth Century New York: Greeley & McElrath, 1845.

Gardner, Howard. Changing Minds: The Art and Science of Changing Our Own and Other People's Minds. Boston: Harvard Business School Press, 2004.

Gienapp, William E. Abraham Lincoln and Civil War America: A Biography. New York: Oxford University Press, 2002.

Gill, Gillian. Nightingales: The Extraordinary Upbringing and Curious Life of Miss Florence Nightingale. New York: Random House Publishing Inc. 2004.

Goodwin, Doris Kearns. Team of Rivals: The Political Genius of Abraham Lincoln. New York: Simon & Schuster, 2006.

Guelzo, Allen C. Abraham Lincoln: Redeemer President. Grand Rapids, MI: William B. Eerdmans Publishing Co., 1999.

Haller, J.S. Intolerable, Excruciating, and Troublesome: Military Ambulance Technology, 1793-1880. Carbondale: Southern University Press, 1992.

Harper, Judith E. Women During The Civil War: An Encyclopedia. New York: Taylor & Francis Group LLC. 2007.

Harvey, Cordelia Adelaide. "Recollections of Hospital Life and Personal Interviews with President Lincoln," Cordelia Adelaide Harvey Papers 1860–1950. _____, "A Wisconsin Woman's Picture of President Lincoln" The Wisconsin Magazine of History 1, no.3, (March 1918).

Herndon, William. "Analysis of the Character of Abraham Lincoln." Herndon's Life of Lincoln, Abraham Lincoln Quarterly Vo1.1 (September 1941), New York: Fawcett Pub. 1961.

Holzer, Harold. Lincoln at Cooper Union: The Speech That Made Abraham Lincoln President New York: Simon & Schuster Inc., 2004.

Hurn, Ethel Alice. "Wisconsin Women in the War Between the States." Wisconsin Historical Society. 6, (May 1911).

Julian, George W. Political Recollections 1840 to 1872. Chicago: Jansen McClure and Co. 1884.

Keen, William W., "Military Surgery in 1861 and in 1918." in The Annals of the American Academy of Political and Social Science. 80, (November 1918).

King, Lester S. M.D. Transformations in American Medicine from Benjamin Rush to William Osler. Baltimore: The Johns Hopkins University Press, 1991.

Kumkale, G. Tarcan., and Dolores Albarracın. "The Sleeper Effect in Persuasion: A Meta-Analytic Review." Psychological Bulletin 130, no.1 (May 2004).

Levine, Robert V. The Power of Persuasion: How We are Bought and Sold. Hoboken, NJ: John Wiley & Sons, 2003.

Livermore, Mary A. My Story of the War. Hartford, CT: a.d. Worthington and Co., 1888.

Love, William D. Wisconsin in the War of the Rebellion. Chicago: Church & Goodwin, 1866.

Maxwell, Richard, and Robert Dickman. The Elements of Persuasion. New York: Harper Collins Publishers, 2007.

Maxwell, William Quentin. Lincoln's Fifth Wheel: The Political History of the United States Sanitary Commission. New York: Longmans, Green and Co., 1956.

McPherson, James. Ordeal by Fire: The Civil War and Reconstruction. 2nd ed. New York: McGraw-Hill, 1992. _____, Abraham Lincoln and the Second American Revolution. New York: Oxford University Press, 1992.

Metchnikoff, Elie. Founders of Modern Medicine: Pasteur, Koch, and Lister. New York: Walden Publications, 1939.

Middleton, William S. M.D., "The Harvey Hospital" Wisconsin Medical Journal. 1, May 1954.

Miller, William Lee. Lincoln's Virtues: An Ethical Biography. New York: A. Knopf, 2002.

Mills, Harry. Artful Persuasion: How to Command Attention, Change Minds, and Influence People. New York: American Management Association, 2000.

Morris, Jan. Lincoln: A Foreigner's Quest. New York: Simon & Schuster, 2000.

Nicolay, Helen. "Lincoln's Cabinet." The Abraham Lincoln Quarterly, 2, (March 1949).

Nevins, Allan. The War for the Union: The Organized War 1863–1864. New York: Charles Scribner's and Sons, 1971.

Patterson, Kelly. Joseph Grenny, Ron McMillan, Al Switzler, Crucial Conversations: Tools for Talking when Stakes are High. New York: McGraw-Hill, 2002.

Penney, Virginia. 500 Employments Adapted To Women, Married or Single. Philadelphia: John E. Potter and Company, 1870.

Reep, Thomas P. Abraham Lincoln and the Frontier Folk of New Salem. Middletown, CT Southfarm Press, 2004.

Roberts, Mary Louise. "True Womanhood Revisited." Journal of Women's History.14, 2002.

Sandburg, Carl. Abraham Lincoln: The War Years, Vol. 4. New York: Harcourt Brace, 1954.

Shenk, Joshua Wolf. Lincoln's Melancholy: How Depression Challenged a President and Fueled His Greatness. New York: Houghton Mifflin Company, 2005.

Simon, Paul. Lincoln's Preparation for Greatness: The Illinois Legislative Years Chicago: University of Illinois Press, 1989.

Simons, Herbert W. Persuasion in Society. Thousand Oaks, CA: Sage Publications Inc. 2001.

Steiner, Paul E. Disease in the Civil War: Natural Biological Warfare in 1861–1865. Springfield, Il: Charles C. Thomas, Publisher, 1968.

Stille, Charles J. "History of the United States Sanitary Commission, the General Report of its Work" During The War of the Rebellion. Philadelphia: J.B. Lippincott & Co., 1866.

Surgeon General, United States Army. The Medical and Surgical History of the War of the Rebellion. Washington: Government Printing Office, (April 1879).

Tarbell, Ida M. "The American Woman." American Magazine.1, (April 1910).

Tripp, C.A. The Intimate World of Abraham Lincoln New York: Simon & Schuster, Inc. 2005.

United States Sanitary Commission, Documents of the U.S. Sanitary Commission. New York: Privately Printed, (1866).

Weik, Jesse. The Real Lincoln: A Portrait. New York: Houghton Mifflin, 1922.

Welter, Barbara. "The Cult of True Womanhood," Dimity Convictions: The American Woman in the Nineteenth Century. Athens: Ohio University Press, 1976.

Whitman, Walt. Memoranda During the War. Bedford, MA: Applewood Books, 1993.

Wiley, Bell Irvin. The Life of Billy Yank: The Common Soldier of the Union. New York: The Bobbs-Merrill Company, Inc., 1952. _____, The Life of Billy Yank: The Common Soldier of the Union Garden City, NJ: Doubleday and Company, Inc. 1972.

Williams, Nancy G. First ladies of Wisconsin: The Governors Wives Kalamazoo: Ana Publishing, 1991.

Wilson, Rufus Rockwell. Intimate Memories of Lincoln. Elmira, NY: Primavera Press, Inc. 1945.

Woodham-Smith, Cecil. Florence Nightingale 1820–1910. New York: McGraw-Hill Book Co. Inc. 1951.

Woodward, Joseph Janvier. M.D. Outlines of the Chief Camp Diseases of the United States Armies. New York: Hafner Publishing Company, 1964.

Yoakam, Doris G. Women's Introduction to the American Platform: In History and Criticism of American Public Address New York: McGraw-Hill, 1943.

Endnotes

Introduction

1 Walt Whitman, Memoranda During the War (Bedford, MA: Applewood Books, 1993), 7.

2 William S. Middleton, "The Harvey Hospital," Wisconsin Medical Journal 1, no.2 (April-May 1954): 279.

The Civil War Medical Dilemma

1 Allan Nevins, The War for the Union: The Organized War 1863-1864 (New York: Charles Scribner's and Sons, 1971), 3: 312

2 Stewart M.Brooks, Civil War Medicine (Springfield, IL: Charles C. Thomas, Publisher, 1966), 63.

3 Ibid., 94.

4   James M. McPherson, Ordeal by Fire: The Civil War and Reconstruction, 2nd ed. (New York: McGraw- Hill, 1992), 385.

5   Elie Metchnikoff, Founders of Modern Medicine: Pasteur, Koch, and Lister (New York: Walden Publications, 1939), 15.

6   William W. Keen, "Military Surgery in 1861,and in 1918," The Annals of the American Academy of Political and Social Science 80 (1918): 14.

7   H.H.Cunningham,Doctors in Grey(Baton Rouge: Louisiana State University Press,1958), 13.

8   Lester S. King, Transformations in American Medicine from Benjamin Rush to William Osler (Baltimore: The Johns Hopkins University Press, 1991), 196.

9   Cunningham, Doctors in Grey, 13.

10 John Duffy, The Healers: The Rise of the Medical Establishment (New York: McGraw-Hill Book Company, 1976), 208-09.

11 George Worthington Adams, Doctors in Blue: The Medical History of the Union Army in the Civil War (New York: Henry Schumann, 1952), 4.

12 Ibid., 4-5.

13 J. S. Haller, Intolerable, Excruciating, and Troublesome: Military Ambulance Technology, 1793-

1880 (Carbondale: Southern University Press, 1992), 4.

14 Brooks, Civil War Medicine, 74.
15 Ibid., 75.
16 Ibid., 99.
17 Ibid., 78.
18 Keen, "1861 and in 1918," 14.
19 Brooks, Civil War Medicine, 97.
20 United States Sanitary Commission, Documents of the U.S. Sanitary Commission (New York: Privately printed, 1866), 40: 33, 17: 33.
21 Ibid., 17: 53.
22 Louisa May Alcott, Hospital Sketches and Camp and Fireside Stories (Boston: Roberts Brothers, 1869), 98.
23 Ibid., 98.
24 Joseph Javier Woodward, Outlines of the Chief Camp Diseases of the United States Armies (New York: Hafner Publishing Company, 1964), 24.
25 Ibid., 23.
26 Paul E. Steiner, Disease in the Civil War: Natural Biological Warfare in 1861-1865 (Springfield, IL: Charles C. Thomas, Publisher, 1968), 8.
27 Ibid., 27.

28 Ibid., 33-34.

29 Woodward, Outlines of the Chief Camp Diseases, 30.

30 Surgeon General, United States Army, The Medical and Surgical History of the War of the Rebellion (Washington: Government Printing Office), Medical 2, no.3 (1879): 649.

31 Woodward, Chief Camp Diseases, 26-29.

32 Ibid., 31-32.

33 Documents of the U.S. Sanitary Commission, 17: 3, 4.

34 Ibid., 17: 1.

35 Cunningham, Doctors in Grey, 165.

36 John D. Billings, Hardtack and Coffee: The Unwritten Story of Army Life, ed. Richard Harwell (Chicago: he Lakeside Press, R.R Donnelly and Sons Company, 1960), 110.

37 Documents of the U.S. Sanitary Commission, 17: 11.

38 Ibid., 17: 4.

39 Ibid., 17: 5.

40 Cunningham, Doctors in Grey, 167.

41 Bell Irvin Wiley, The Life of Billy Yank: The Common Soldier of the Union (New York: The Bobbs- Merrill Company, Inc., 1952), 128.

42 Documents of the U.S. Sanitary Commission, 17: 3.

43   Ibid., 17: 2.

44   William Quentin Maxwell, Lincoln's Fifth Wheel: The Political History of the United States Sanitary Commission (New York: Longmans, Green and Co., 1956), 5.

45   Charles J. Stille, History of the United States Sanitary Commission, Being the General Report of its Work During The War of the Rebellion (Philadelphia: J.B. Lippincott & Co., 1866), 29-30.

46   Documents of the U.S. Sanitary Commission, 22: 4.

47   Drew Gilpin Faust, This Republic Of Suffering: Death and the American Civil War (New York: Alfred A. Knopf, 2008), 4.

Abraham Lincoln: Leadership and Character Analysis

1   William E. Gienapp, Abraham Lincoln and Civil War America A Biography (New York: Oxford University Press, 2002), ix.

2   Ibid., x.

3   Ibid.,

4   Issac Arnold, The Life of Abraham Lincoln 1884 (Lincoln: University of Nebraska Press, 1994), 81.

5   Jesse Weik, The Real Lincoln: A Portrait (New York: Houghton Mifflin, 1992), 112.

6   William Herndon, "Analysis of the Character of Abraham Lincoln," Abraham Lincoln Quarterly 1, no.3 (May 1941): 371.

7   Ibid., 372.

8   Allen C. Guelzo, Abraham Lincoln: Redeemer President (Grand Rapids, MI: William B. Eerdmans Publishing Co., 1999), 164.

9   Joshua Wolf Shenk, Lincoln's Melancholy: How Depression Challenged a President and Fueled His Greatness (New York: Houghton Mifflin Company, 2005), 215.

10 Ibid., 156.

11 Ibid., 200-01.

12 Ibid., 215.

13 Doris Kearns Goodwin, Team of Rivals: The Political Genius of Abraham Lincoln (New York: Simon & Schuster, 2006), xvi.

14 Ibid.

15 Ibid., 304.

16 Michael Burlingame, The Inner World of Abraham Lincoln (Chicago: University of Illinois Press, 1994), 314.

17 Thomas P. Reep, Abraham Lincoln and the Frontier Folk of New Salem (Middletown, CT: Southfarm Press, 2002), 130

18 James M. McPherson, Abraham Lincoln and the Second American Revolution (New York: Oxford University Press, 1992), 93.

19 Allen G. Guelzo, "Holland's Informants: The Construction of Josiah Holland's Life of Abraham Lincoln," Journal of the Abraham Lincoln Association 23, no.1, (Winter 2002): 53.

20 Paul M. Angle, ed., Abraham Lincoln by Some Men who Knew Him (Chicago: Ayer Company, 1950), 106.

21 Rufus Rockwell Wilson, Intimate Memories of Lincoln (Elmira, NY: The Primavera Press, Inc. 1945), 406.

22 Francis B. Carpenter, Six Months at the White House with Abraham Lincoln (New York: Published by Hurd and Houghton, 1867), 286.

23 Ibid., 337.

24 William H. Herndon and Jesse W. Weik, Herndon's Life of Lincoln (New York: Fawcett Publishing inc. 1961), 480.

25 Herndon and Weik, Life of Lincoln, 487-88.

26 Guelzo, Abraham Lincoln: Redeemer President, 463.

27 William E. Doster, Lincoln and Episodes of the Civil War (New York: G. P.Putnam's & Sons, 1915), 17.

28 William Lee Miller, Lincoln's Virtues: an Ethical Biography (New York: Alfred A. Knopf, 2002), 406.

29 Carl Sandburg, Abraham Lincoln: The War Years 4, (New York: Harcourt Brace Inc.1954), 80.

30 Maunsell B. Field, Memories of Many Men and Some Women (New York: Harpers,1874), 112.

31 C. A. Tripp, The Intimate World of Abraham Lincoln (New York: Simon & Schuster, Inc. 2005), 80.

32 Ward Hill Lamon, James A. Rawley, Dorothy Lamon Teillard, Recollections of Abraham Lincoln (Lincoln: University of Nebraska Press, 1994), 124-25.

33 Roy P.Basler, ed., The Collected Works of Abraham Lincoln. (New Brunswick, NJ: Rutgers University Press, 1958), 2: 208.

34 Ibid., 209.

35 Bell Irvin Wiley, The Life of Billy Yank: The Common Soldier of the Union (Garden City, NJ: Doubleday and Company, Inc. 1972), 216.

36 L. E. Chittenden, Personal Reminiscences: Including Lincoln and Others 1840-1890 (New York: Richmond, Croscup and Company, 1893), 406.

37 Jan Morris, Lincoln: A Foreigner's Quest (New York: Simon & Schuster, 2000), 138.

38 Ibid., 142.

Cordelia Harvey: Nineteenth-century Humanitarian

1 Cecil Woodham-Smith, Florence Nightingale, 1820-1910 (New York: McGraw-Hill Book Co. Inc 1951), 174.

2 L. P. Brockett and Mary C. Vaughn, Woman's Work in the Civil War: A Record of Heroism, Patriotism and Patience (Philadelphia: Zeigler, McCurdy & Co., 1867), 262.

3 William D. Love, Wisconsin in the War of the Rebellion (Chicago: Church and Goodwin, 1866), 104.

4   S. Margaret Fuller, Women in The Nineteenth Century (New York: Greeley & McElrath, 160 Nassau Street, 1845), 218.

5   Ibid., 223.

6   Mary Louise Roberts, "True Womanhood Revisited," Journal of Women's History 14, (May 2002): 150-85.

7   Barbara Welter, Dimity Convictions: The American Woman in the Nineteenth Century (Athens: Ohio University Press, 1976), 21.

8   Ibid., 40.

9   Doris G. Yoakam, Women's Introduction to the American Platform: In History and Criticism of American Public Address (New York: McGraw-Hill, 1943), 153.

10 Kenneth Cmiel, Democratic Eloquence: The Fight over Popular Speech in Nineteenth-Century America (New York: William Morrow and Company, Inc., 1990), 70.

11 Ibid., 71.

12 Nancy G. Williams, First ladies of Wisconsin: The Governors Wives (Kalamazoo: Ana Publishing, 1991), 53.

13 Virginia Penney, 500 Employments Adapted To Women, Married or Single (Philadelphia: John E. Potter and Company, 1870), 44.

14 Fuller, Women in the Nineteenth-Century, 223.

15 "Death of Governor Louis Harvey," Chicago Daily Tribune, April 26, 1862, sec. 2.

16 George W. Julian, Political Recollections 1840 to 1872 (Chicago: Jansen McClure and Co. 1884), 362.

17 William S. Middleton, "The Harvey Hospital" Wisconsin Medical Journal 5, no. 2 (April-May 1954): 231.

18 Ethel Alice Hurn, "Wisconsin Women in the War Between the States," Wisconsin History Commission Original Papers 1, no 6 (May 1911): 118.

19 William DeLoss Love, Wisconsin in the War of the Rebellion, (Chicago: Church and Goodman Publishers, 1866), 1050.

20 Ibid., 1050.

21 Ibid., 1051.

22 Ibid.

23 Ida M. Tarbell, "The American Woman," American Magazine, (April 1910), 811.

24 Mary A. Livermore, My Story of the War (Hartford, CT: A.D. Worthington and Co., 1888), 129.

25 Middleton, "The Harvey Hospital," 232.

26 Cordelia Adelaide Harvey, "Recollections of Hospital Life and Personal Interviews with President Lincoln," Cordelia Adelaide Harvey

Papers, State Historical Society of Wisconsin, Madison.

27 Gillian Gill, Nightingales: The Extraordinary Upbringing and Curious Life of Miss Florence Nightingale (New York: Random House Publishing Inc. 2004), 334.

28 Ibid., 335.

29 Middleton, "The Harvey Hospital," 232.

30 Ibid.

31 Ibid., 233.

32 Harvey "Recollections of Hospital Life," 16.

33 Drew Gilpin Faust, This Republic Of Suffering: Death and the American Civil War (New York: Alfred A. Knopf, 2008), 209.

34 Kate Cumming, Journal of a Confederate Nurse (Baton Rouge: Louisiana State University Press, 1959),15.

35 Ethel Alice Hurn, "Wisconsin Women in the War Between the States," 126.

36 Harvey, "Recollections of Hospital Life,"

Harvey's Campaign Strategy for the Union Soldiers

1 William S. Middleton, "The Harvey Hospital" Wisconsin Medical Journal 4, no. 2 (April-May 1954): 232.

2 Cordelia Adelaide Harvey, "Recollections of Hospital Life and Personal Interviews with President Lincoln," Cordelia Adelaide Harvey Papers, State Historical Society of Wisconsin, Madison. 19.

3 Ibid., 4.

4 Judith E. Harper, Women During The Civil War: An Encyclopedia (New York: Taylor & Francis Group LLC. 2007),180.

5 Harvey, "Recollections of Hospital Life," 4.

6 Ibid., 5.

7 Ibid., 6.

8 Ibid., 11.

9 Ibid., 2.

10 Middleton, "The Harvey Hospital," 277.

11 Drew Gilpin Faust, This Republic Of Suffering: Death and the American Civil War (New York: Alfred A. Knopf, 2008), 61.

12 Middleton, "The Harvey Hospital," 232.

13 Ibid., 19.

14 Ibid., 15.

15 Ibid., 16.

16 Ibid.

17 Ibid., 17.

18 Ibid.

19 Ibid., 18.

20 Ibid., 19.

21 Ibid.

22 Ibid.

23 Ibid.

24 Ibid., 24.

25 Ibid., 25.

26 Cordelia A. P. Harvey, "A Wisconsin Woman's Picture of President Lincoln," The Wisconsin Magazine of History 1, no. 3 (March 1918), 248.

27 Ibid., 249.

28 Ibid.

29 Ibid.

30 Ibid.

31 Ibid.

32 Ibid., 250.

33 Ibid.

34 Ibid.
35 Ibid.
36 Ibid.
37 Ibid.
38 Ibid., 251.
39 Ibid., 252.
40 Ibid., 243.
41 Ibid.
42 Ibid.
43 Ibid.
44 Ibid.
45 Ibid.
46 Ibid., 249.
47 Ibid., 252.
48 Ibid.
49 Ibid.
50 Ethel Alice Hurn, "Wisconsin Women in the War Between the States," Wisconsin Historical Society (May 1911): 143.
51 Middleton, "The Harvey Hospital," 232.
52 William D. Love, Wisconsin in the War of the Rebellion (Chicago: Church and Goodwin, 1866), 109.

53   Kenneth Cmiel, Democratic Eloquence: The Fight over Popular Speech in Nineteenth-Century America (New York: William Morrow and Company, Inc., 1990), 13.

54   Ibid., 25.

Conclusion: Theoretical Analysis

1   S. Margaret Fuller, Women in The Nineteenth Century (New York: Greeley & McElrath, 160 Nassau Street, 1845), 220.

2   Kelly Patterson, Joseph Grenny, Ron McMillan, Al Switzler, Crucial Conversations Tools for Talking When Stakes are High (New York: McGraw-Hill, 2002), 27.

3   Ibid., 30.

4   Cordelia A. P. Harvey, "A Wisconsin Woman's Picture of President Lincoln" The Wisconsin Magazine of History 1 no. 3 (March 1918), 250.

5   Patterson, Crucial Conversations, 151.

6   Harvey, "A Wisconsin Woman's Picture," 251.

7   Robert B. Cialdini, Influence: The Psychology of Persuasion (New York: William Morrow and Co.2000), 4.

8   Ibid., 60.

9   Harry Mills, Artful Persuasion: How to Command Attention, Change Minds, and Influence People (New York: American Management Association, 2000), 59.

10 Paul Simon, Lincoln's Preparation for Greatness: The Illinois Legislative Years (Chicago: University of Illinois Press, 1989), 14.

11 Mills, Artful Persuasion, 60.

12 Richard Maxwell and Robert Dickman, The Elements of Persuasion (New York: Harper Collins Publishers, 2007), 27.

13 Robert V. Levine, The Power of Persuasion: How We are Bought and Sold (Hoboken, NJ: John Wiley& Sons, 2003), 43-44.

14 Timothy C. Brock and Melanie Colette Green, Persuasion: Psychological insights and Perspectives (Thousand Oaks, CA: Sage Publications Inc. 2005), 107.

15 Herbert W. Simons, Persuasion in Society (Thousand Oaks, CA: Sage Publications Inc. 2001), 170.

16 G. Tarcan Kumkale and Dolores Albarracin, "The Sleeper Effect in Persuasion: A Meta-Analytic Review" Psychological Bulletin 130, no.1 (2004): 143-72.

www.ingramcontent.com/pod-product-compliance
Lightning Source LLC
LaVergne TN
LVHW091555060526
838200LV00036B/848